I
AM
A DRUG
LORD

I AM A DRUG LORD

THE LAST CONFESSION OF A REAL-LIFE UNDERWORLD KINGPIN

ANONYMOUS

WELBECK

Published by Welbeck
An imprint of Welbeck Non-Fiction Limited,
part of Welbeck Publishing Group.
20 Mortimer Street,
London W1T 3JW

First published by Welbeck in 2021

A CIP catalogue record for this book is available from the British Library

ISBN
Paperback – 9781787398207
eBook – 9781787398214

Typeset by seagulls.net
Printed and bound in the UK.

10 9 8 7 6 5 4 3 2 1

www.welbeckpublishing.com

DICTIONARY DEFINITION
OF A DRUG LORD

A criminal who controls the distribution and sale
of large quantities of illegal drugs.

REALITY BITES

This isn't a glamorous story. It's the gritty truth about my life as a drug lord and is filled with good and bad people, because heroes come from the most unlikely of places.

I fell into a situation by complete chance which then changed my life forever. So many of us no doubt wish we'd stopped, taken stock and got the hell out of there before taking the plunge. But this is no time for regrets.

You don't have to be a drug lord or any type of criminal to relate to what you're about to read here, because my story is crammed with life's typical ups and downs. There is one inescapable and brutal truth, though. Narcotics are the toxic fuel that drives the underworld and alters personalities. Drugs poison users, turn dealers into killers and end up costing countless innocent (and not so innocent) people their lives.

That is the reality.

There's no one thing that's true. It's all true.
Ernest Hemingway, *For Whom the Bell Tolls*

AUTHOR'S NOTE –
EYE ON THE WORLD

Everything you're about to read is based on the truth. I've had to be doubly sure there was no way any of the participants in my story were identifiable, or else I would have been putting myself and many others directly in the line of fire – literally. My primary goal with this book has always been to reveal a no-holds-barred confession of my life as a drug lord while at the same time protecting the lives of the many involved.

I felt I needed to be upfront and admit that I've taken some liberties with history in order to disguise illegal stuff that happened throughout my life. No doubt some will use this as an excuse to question the accuracy of my story, but I'd much rather change a few pieces of the jigsaw than face the wrath of real criminals and the police. Ultimately, the ingredients of this book revolve around authentic events, but in order to protect the identity of those involved, names, dates, descriptions and places have had to be altered.

But I hope none of that detracts from the story you're about to read. And I also hope it will serve as a lesson to anyone who thought the world I once inhabited was glamorous and rewarding, because it most certainly was not.

Anonymous, 2021

INTRODUCTION

I am a drug lord. That doesn't make me the most evil person in the world, although some people might think so. But I'm not here to defend my corner. I am what I am.

More importantly, I found myself thrust into the underworld because everything in life is connected. For that reason, you're going to read a fair chunk about my unusual childhood. That doesn't mean tales of child abuse and other horrors, because this is no misery memoir. But my early life was so bizarre that it helped shape my life in all sorts of ways. I was brought up in a laid-back, hippy-like environment where you just went with the flow. The traditional elements of an upbringing were turned upside down from an early age, and that undoubtedly provided me with an inner calmness, which enabled me to cope with pretty much anything.

If you're expecting a book that dissects the rights and wrongs of the underworld, then stick to more traditional true crime stories, because this one doesn't preach or lecture. It's a relatable story for people of all persuasions. My life has been multi-layered and filled with dramas and close shaves, but

I've always managed to retain a sense of perspective, despite everything that's been thrown at me.

There may even be some omissions that will irritate the real criminals among you. But it's more important that this story works for everyone on *all* levels than to worry about the sensitivities of a few wannabe gangsters. I toned down some scenes because that old phrase "stranger than fiction" really did apply to certain aspects of my life as a drug lord. These extreme and bloody events – which many would have struggled to suspend disbelief long enough to accept – are the real and disturbing consequences of my actions.

I will warn you, I'm not a scholar. I had little formal education during my childhood, so what you see is what you read in my world. There may even be a few clunky lines that have slipped through the editing process. But the essential, omnipresent ingredient that ties my story together is the pace of my life as a drug lord. Chaos and immense danger drive this story to its bloody conclusion.

Ultimately, I've tried to provide an entertaining story that will hopefully get you turning pages at much the same pace as my own life evolved. Then, at least, you'll get to the end. The bloody, chaotic end.

So, if you're now ready… let's begin.

PROLOGUE – THE STORM

Glistening waves as big as two-story houses swept towards me under the hazy moonlight, flickering in and out of the dark clouds drifting above me. Each of those waves scooped me up and threw me across the sea so ferociously that I felt dizzy from it all. It was like being on an aquatic roller coaster ride, except all I had was a flimsy, threadbare old lifejacket to keep me afloat. But despite that, each time I was pulled beneath the surface, it felt as if I might not come up again.

Then – with the swelling sea thundering and exploding all around me – I heard the unmistakable sound of wood splitting as the full, brutal force of the storm began to rip apart the boat I'd just been swept off. As the frothy, luminous grey crest of those waves dipped and weaved around me, I could just make out the bright yellow hull of the vessel as it twisted up into the air, almost like an orca whale, before crashing back into the sea. The storm was dragging me further and further away from the boat and the rest of the crew.

When another vast wave tossed me up towards the dark, patchy sky, I noticed a flickering searchlight hundreds of yards away. It disappeared again and I thought maybe I'd imagined it. Moments later, I could just make out the bow of another boat a long way off in the distance before it dipped behind yet another rolling wave. The glaring beam of its searchlight reappeared and panned eerily across the water's surface. The other boat seemed to be edging towards me, but it was impossible to be sure because I was being dragged in all directions by the fury of the sea.

I shouted and waved the next time the other vessel came into view, knowing full well the chances of anyone noticing me were slim. Another huge wave crashed over the top of me, and I was dragged beneath the surface for a few moments until popping up again, thanks entirely to my life jacket.

As I bobbed around on the surface in the darkness, I looked again for the yellow boat I'd been travelling on. It was nowhere to be seen. Then, suddenly, the beam of the powerful searchlight almost blinded me. The noise of diesel engines got louder and I realized the other vessel was much closer now.

As it came fully into view, the boat leaned to one side before skimming over a huge wave, which sent its bow crashing down so deep into the water that its shiny twin propellers were exposed in the bluey moonlight. The hull smashed back into the water with a huge crack as the engines continued throbbing.

The blinding beam of the searchlight returned and panned across me during a brief lull in the huge waves. As the boat's engines powered it towards me, I noticed its green and white hull just as another vast wave hit the vessel, tossing it in the air and sending that spotlight shooting erratically up into the bleak sky, leaving me once again in almost total darkness. I had no idea if it would ever reach me.

Remembering how I came to be in those angry seas in the first place, I frantically looked around, hoping the others from my boat would suddenly surface alongside me. As the green and white boat continued its struggle through the relentless storm towards me, I slumped deeper into my life jacket, afraid to face the reality of what was happening all around.

The searchlight flickered across my face as the approaching boat criss-crossed the waves. That's when the sound of those powerful engines took me back to where this story really begins, just a few miles from where the storm now raged.

ACT I

A STRANGE CHILDHOOD

1958–1975

CHAPTER ONE
TRANSLUCENT

The sound of diesel engines just above me was muffled by the warm sea water as I drifted through a school of jellyfish gliding past me like dancing ghosts. I must have been about 10 feet under the water and had no idea of whether anyone knew I'd just fallen in and couldn't swim. Yet it felt strangely liberating, as the adults who'd featured in the first four years of my life were nowhere to be seen.

I remember floating randomly past more of those elegant, translucent Medusa jellyfish, who seemed to thrive on peace and tranquillity. Looking back on it now, I realize they must have been in some kind of zen-like state as they drifted past me. None of them stung me, but then why would they? I wasn't bothering them and they weren't bothering me.

I'd just fallen into the Mediterranean Sea from one of the old fishing boats that brought visitors to my parents' favourite beach on the island of Ibiza. We'd been mooring up alongside the jetty after a typically choppy ride from the nearest town with my uncle, who was visiting from London. My mother and father had just moved to the island after he lost his job as a newspaper reporter in London. It was the summer of 1962 and Ibiza wasn't very well known, just a sparsely populated island off the coast of mainland Spain. My mother and uncle had first discovered it more than 20 years earlier when they fought with the Republican's International Brigades against the nationalist forces of Fascist leader General Francisco Franco during the Spanish Civil War between 1936 and 1939.

I always looked forward to those boat journeys with the fishermen so much that I'd hardly be able to sleep the night before for the excitement and anticipation. To a shy and solitary 4-year-old more used to adults than other children, that trip represented a thrilling adventure to a secret place where I could then be as free as the Medusa and all the other creatures that lived in and around the beach.

On that particular morning, I'd over-confidently chosen to jump from the edge of the fishing boat onto the jetty before the crew had thrown a rope to secure the vessel. A wave had rocked the boat at that moment, and I went straight into the clear blue sea.

I remember looking up at the sky as I fell backwards into the water with a soft plop. I later discovered that my badly hungover parents hadn't noticed I wasn't on the boat anymore. My uncle had been sitting opposite them looking down at the Medusa jellyfish when he heard the splash, saw me sinking beneath the waves and jumped into the water after me.

I remember hearing the muffled gurgling sound of the bubbles he created above me and looking up and seeing nothing but the scuffed soles of his black leather shoes. No one wore shoes like that in Ibiza. It was either flip-flops or espadrilles made out of rope. I felt a hand clutching the back of my tee-shirt as my uncle began to pull me gradually up to the surface.

Two more pairs of hands appeared just beneath the surface of the sea from the edge of the fishing boat. They grabbed me roughly and hauled me up onto the wooden deck, where I was pushed onto my side and all the water I'd consumed gushed out of me.

Then someone yelled: "Where's that guy gone?"

This was followed by my mother's familiar voice: "El no puede nadar. El no puede nadar." (He can't swim. He can't swim).

It took everyone on board a few moments to realize she was talking about my uncle, who was still in the water, not me.

As I was sitting up, four of the fishing boat crew dived into the sea. I remember squinting over the edge of the vessel into the water as their silhouettes swam through schools of yet more jellyfish gliding all around the vessel. Below them was the blurred image of my uncle drifting downwards into the deeper, dark blue water before disappearing under the hull.

A few moments passed as we all peered so frantically over the edge of the boat that it leaned precariously to one side. My mother looked shell-shocked, while my father seemed irritated and stared up at the sky as if he didn't really care.

Suddenly, all four fishermen burst back onto the surface with broad smiles on their faces, clutching my uncle. They pushed him up into the arms of others on the deck. One of them straddled him and began thumping his chest until his eyes opened. My uncle looked across at me, smiled and then winked.

A few minutes later, as we walked down the beach, my parents were arguing about whose fault it was that I'd almost drowned. When I tugged on my mother's bright green tie-dye cotton dress to stop her shouting, she ignored me and continued bickering with my father. Not for the first or last time, they were in a world of their own.

After we finally reached their favourite, deserted spot in the far corner of the beach, my mother pulled a transparent brown plastic bottle out of her straw bag and gave it to me. As I obediently began slapping greasy coconut oil on her already bronzed and sinewy back, I looked up at the beach bar behind us where my uncle and another man were deep in conversation. My uncle had been visiting the island that weekend attending to "some important business". It was only many years later I discovered what that actually meant.

* * *

That evening, my uncle came into my bedroom to read me a couple of night-time stories, which he always did in a very theatrical and entertaining voice. He usually renamed the main character after me in each book.

He sat down on the edge of my bed that night, about to start reading the first book, when he asked me to guess what he had in his clenched hand. I didn't know what to say, so I tried to prise it open. But he kept it closed tightly until I gave up. Then his fingers slowly opened to reveal a tiny metal toy car, which I'd dropped in the sea when I'd fallen in earlier that morning. I was so happy he'd found it that I gave him a big hug. I remember feeling just about as secure as any child could feel at that moment.

But that feeling didn't last long. I got up next morning and dashed into his bedroom, only to find his bed empty and that he'd gone. When I asked my mother whether he was coming back, she looked gloomily at me and complained that he hadn't even said goodbye before leaving.

* * *

Not surprisingly, my parents became obsessed with me learning how to swim after that. Throughout my childhood, my mother constantly harked back to that day when I'd almost drowned. Later, I realized it gave her an excuse to put my uncle on a pedestal for having saved me despite not being able to swim himself.

He would go on to reappear occasionally through my early childhood, emerging eventually as a larger-than-life yet mystical figure. Back then, I didn't see him often, which made his visits to Ibiza even more firmly imprinted in my mind.

But it wasn't until many years later that I found out who he really was.

* * *

My father later told me that my mother began having nips of gin with her coffee most mornings around the time I nearly drowned because it helped kill the pain of what she called her "gammy leg". I never understood why she called it a leg, because she didn't have one at all, just a stump above where her knee would have been. I was too young back then to know how she'd come to lose her leg. It was just one of many things that happened to her before I turned up in this world.

My mother had originally arrived in London from central Europe after the end of the Second World War in 1945 and met my father, fell in love and married. But they were in their late thirties by the time I was born in 1958, which was quite old to have children back then.

During the early years of my childhood, I mistakenly blamed myself for my mother's missing leg after becoming convinced she'd lost it giving birth to me when I overheard her telling one friend how difficult her pregnancy had been. She hadn't been well treated in hospital in London when I was born, thanks to a combination of that already missing leg and her strange foreign accent, which some days sounded French and other days seemed like a combination of German and Spanish, depending on who she was talking to at the time.

After that, if anyone asked my mother how she lost her leg, the most she'd say was "La Guerra" (the war), although more often she simply ignored the question. Back in those days, women didn't fight on the frontline in conflicts, so her response did provoke quite a few raised eyebrows.

My mother eventually applied for a prosthetic leg after one sympathetic doctor convinced her it might help ease her pain and make raising a child a lot easier. But the National Health specialist who had to sign off on it then announced that those injured in the Spanish Civil War were not being given priority for prosthetics because there were still thousands of British ex-service men and women and Blitz bombing victims from the First and Second World War who required a new limb.

Despite her missing leg, my mother still attracted admiring glances from men and women, which must have been hard on my father because he often seemed to be in her shadow. She was tall and statuesque and had dark red wavy hair that especially stood out on Ibiza where most people had dark hair. Her strong, angular face had a splattering of freckles, and she usually wore a little eye shadow. But it was her shoulders I remember most, as I spent so many hours smothering coconut oil on them in scorching heat.

There's not much else to say about my life before I reached the age of four, because my memories rely on the unreliable word of the adults around me, who were often drunk at the time. What I do know is that just after my fourth birthday my parents had to sell their house in West London after my father was fired from his newspaper job for making up an interview with a well-known politician. I think he got a small pay-off but then went and lost it all in a casino. That's when my mother decided we'd all be better off living in Ibiza, although most of the people they knew in London didn't know where the island was at that time. I'm not entirely sure what we were living off, but we seemed to just get through.

They'd already had a villa there for five years. Back in those days, the island – about 12 miles wide and 21 miles long – had just one pot-holed main road running through the middle of it that was used by far more horses and carts than motor vehicles. Ibiza's charm was that it felt as if it was stuck in a time warp back then.

CHAPTER TWO
PLAYA SECRETA

While there had been post-war rationing across Europe throughout the 1950s and into the early 1960s, on Ibiza you could buy a bottle of beer for ten pence and gin was less than a pound a bottle. Food was even cheaper, with fish being the staple diet, and there was a plentiful supply of rice, thanks to the carefully cultivated rice fields on the south of the island, which had helped the locals avoid starvation during the civil war. Rare shipments of meat occasionally turned up by cargo boats from the mainland and there were always a lot of wild rabbits and some goats to eat. But Ibiza's staple diet tended to be fish and rice mainly.

The ramshackle villa where we lived was shaped like a small tower and had been built in the middle of a deserted plain a couple of miles from the nearest pueblo (village). It could only be reached via a rocky track using a horse and cart that was driven by a neighbouring farmer, who owned all the land around the villa.

But it was the playa secreta (secret beach) where I'd almost drowned that had a far bigger impact on my childhood... and on the rest of my life.

It was owned and run by a New Zealander, who'd fought alongside my mother and uncle during the Spanish Civil

War. During that war they'd all been locked up in a makeshift prison camp on Ibiza run by the nationalists' feared paramilitary force, the Guardia Civil. The camp was located close to the deserted swamplands where all that rice was grown, just a few miles outside the capital, Ibiza Old Town.

The Guardia Civil were Franco's most feared and hated paramilitary force. He specifically developed them from a police force first launched in the mid-1800s into his tool to strike terror into citizens during and after the civil war. Following his victory in 1939, Franco had assured Spain's shell-shocked citizens that the Guardia Civil would revert to being a standard police force, but they continued to be his eyes and ears throughout his 40-year reign as leader of Spain.

Yet despite all this, a small group of those same foreigners Franco had loathed so much for daring to fight against his nationalist forces decided to settle on Ibiza and ignore the painful memories of one of the most bloody conflicts of the twentieth century.

In the late 1940s, my mother's New Zealander friend paid the Guardia Civil a few hundred dollars for an abandoned village that they'd taken over during the war. It was near the prison camp where my mother and he had been held captive. The village had been used by guards between shifts in the camp, and prisoners would be dragged to its square where – right in front of the church – they'd be interrogated and sometimes executed if they did not co-operate with the fascist authorities. The Guardia Civil had deliberately blown up the road into the nearest town to stop anyone going into the village following the end of the civil war.

The New Zealander had originally purchased the village with the intention of demolishing it to erase all the painful memories. Then he noticed the deserted beach in front of it and opted to stay. He eventually decided to leave the village standing as a memorial to all his late comrades who'd died on the island and elsewhere in Spain throughout the bloody three-year conflict. The secret beach became a place where many of those civil war veterans could gather peacefully, swap war stories and get blind drunk without having to face the Franco supporters who ran the island following his victory.

Besides the New Zealander and his wife, there was a civil war vet nicknamed American Joe. He ran a small commune about two miles inland from the secret beach on the land owned by the New Zealander. I later learned American Joe had been a sniper during the civil war after earlier having been a US secret service bodyguard to President Franklin D. Roosevelt in the mid-1930s.

The secret beach itself was rarely crowded because it could only be reached by boat. The only other visitors tended to be adventurous European traveller types, many of whom seemed to be running away from something. Ibiza wasn't a party island like it is today. The few foreigners living there at that time were mainly broke artists and writers residing in rundown villas and fincas similar to my parents' home. Many of them seemed to drink at the New Zealander's beach bar during the first 10 years of my life. The foreign residents like my parents might have looked more colourful and glamorous than the locals, but they actually had little money to show for it.

As the island became more popular, hole-in-the-wall bars hidden down Ibiza Old Town's maze of narrow alleyways began to open, although many of the bar owners had to pay protection money to local criminals to avoid being put out of business.

The majority of locals at this time lived in small white stone houses, usually deep in the campo – countryside – where many had fled from the violence and turmoil inside Ibiza's towns and villages during and after the civil war. Gradually, some of the new foreign residents began also setting up homes in the ancient quarter of Ibiza Old Town, rather than on isolated plots of land like my parents had done. Bars painted in psychedelic colours started popping up around the Old Town port. Clothes shops and stalls sold flowery shirts, tie-dye wraps, multi-coloured espadrilles and the tight-fitting loon pants that were the most classic hippy trademark of all back then.

Many of the foreign men on the island had grown their hair much longer than the macho Spanish males, who still considered long hair to be effeminate. Yet a lot of the hippy types arriving on Ibiza at that time were often old enough – like my parents – to have fought in the civil war and Second World War.

Throughout this period, many of the locals treated us as if we didn't really exist. They rarely smiled in our direction, apart from the fishermen who crewed the boat that took us to the secret beach most mornings. Many loathed my mother and her International Brigades friends for daring to have stood up to Franco's fascists, although the war had been over for more than 20 years. She'd fought alongside other foreigners in some of that conflict's most bloody battles on mainland Spain.

This was the atmosphere in Ibiza in the early 1960s. It was a third-world land filled with contradictions, and those deep scars from the civil war continued to cause political and ideological divisions, as they did throughout the rest of spain. But it's important to also point out that a lot of the anger wasn't always caused by political differences. Quite a number of families used the civil war as an excuse to settle old scores between feuding locals.

Yet the ghosts of so many atrocities committed on Ibiza had done nothing to put off my mother, my uncle and the friends they'd fought alongside, including the New Zealander and American Joe. But maybe that's not such a surprise when you consider what a strange yet entrancing place it was back then. Also, most people seemed to be drunk morning, noon and night, and my parents were no exception to that rule.

In fairness to my mother, she was exhausted for a lot of my childhood because she only had the use of a flimsy walking stick to enable her to get about. Her energy levels only soared when she had a drink in her hand. She liked to sing around the house, and that could mean anything from Ray Charles to Sarah Vaughan. Much of that music became the soundtrack to my early life on Ibiza.

I should have been jealous of other kids with brothers and sisters, but I wasn't, because I absorbed everything around me, both good and bad, and that provided me with much more to think about than any friend could.

Just a few years before we moved to Ibiza full time in 1962, Franco had decided to try and improve the country's struggling finances by encouraging mass tourism to all of Spain's sunniest coastal areas, including the Balearic Islands of Ibiza, Mallorca and Menorca. Franco initially neglected Ibiza in favour of his favourite Balearic Island, Mallorca, which he designated to be the first one to be developed for the tourist invasion that he rightly predicted would save his nation's economy.

Franco encouraged the rest of the world to believe that Spain was rapidly modernizing and had put its internal differences behind it. A secretive clean-up operation was launched to hide some of the most obvious evidence of his brutal dictatorship, so all prison camps were hastily flattened. However, it soon became clear to Franco and his tourism minister that most visitors to Spain only really cared that it was cheap and sunny.

* * *

The secret beach itself was 500 metres wide and bordered by high jagged-edged rocks on both sides. I was in bare feet the first time I climbed those rocks. When I got back to where my parents were sunbathing, my mother noticed a trail of my bloody footprints in the sand, as the rocks had cut the soles of my feet to ribbons. I remember her frantically hobbling around as she covered up the blood with handfuls of sand. It wasn't until much later that I realized the random sight of blood in the sand had brought back so many painful memories for her.

The reminders and the contradictions of the civil war seemed omnipresent for my mother, even at the secret beach. High up behind it was a small hillside pine forest where locals would often go hunting for rabbits and wild boar. The noise of their gun blasts in fast succession echoing across the bay would terrify my mother so much that she'd often get my father to fetch her a sangria laced with gin from the beach bar to try and calm her nerves.

The New Zealander who owned the beach also ran that ramshackle bar which overlooked it. Most mornings the fishermen – whose boats brought us to the beach each morning – would sup on a beer and a cognac in the shade. Sometimes they drunkenly dropped peseta coins in the thick sand under their feet at the bar and didn't bother to pick them up. I'd watch them from a nearby wall under the shade of a huge eucalyptus tree until they'd gone and then sneak in and scramble around on my hands and knees plucking coins out of the sand.

One time, I was digging through the sand with my bare hands when I noticed a pair of raggedly flip-flops and a shadow looming over me. It was the New Zealander, and he twisted his foot into the sand so that a couple more coins popped up, almost magically. On other occasions, he'd slap peseta coins down on the bar with the side featuring the crow-like head of General Franco on display. Then he'd smash each one with his fist so hard that it would fly off the bar and down into the sand on the floor.

* * *

When I was five my mother enrolled me in a local school. I already spoke pidgin Spanish, so could communicate with people, but the other kids ignored me because I wasn't one of them. I was so self-sufficient by this stage that I brushed it all off and got on with living in my own little world. I faced a lot of bullying at that school because of my mother's participation in the civil war and the fact that I was a foreigner. Often,

I was thrown out of games of football on dusty pitches after the other kids called me a useless gringo.

But I didn't really need school. I ended up learning more by reading British newspapers than I ever did in class, although they didn't reach the island until at least five days after publication. My father would buy one most mornings as we walked through the village on the way to get the fishing boat to the secret beach. I'd then wait patiently for him to read it on the beach before sitting under the shade of a tree and catching up on world affairs.

We eventually got a dog my parents called Mister Chamberlain after the pacifist prime minister who took Britain into a world war with Hitler immediately after the civil war had ended. Mister Chamberlain was a *podenco ibicenco*, a breed unique to the island, with sharp, sphinx-type ears and the lean stance of a greyhound.

I learned more about trust from my dog than from any human beings as a child. Mister Chamberlain always came to me when I called. He loved me unconditionally and so I always returned my trust to him in bucketloads. But all that did was fool me into believing humans were the same, which was definitely not the case.

Sometimes when I was out wandering the hills with my dog, I'd come across old bullet casings. I never told my mother, but I was collecting them to sell in town to scrap metal dealers who toured the streets in a horse and cart looking for old pieces of metal. Mister Chamberlain dragged me all over Ibiza. We'd walk for hours and hours through fields and olive groves, across small mountain passes and along the edge of high cliffs that skirted much of the island.

My parents warned me that some areas were still strongholds for many of Franco's most ardent fascist supporters. My mother said they might not take kindly to a foreign boy wandering through their village, especially if they realized I was related to her.

One time three much older boys appeared on the outskirts of a village and began throwing rocks at myself and Mister Chamberlain. I eventually set him on them, and he bit one of them on his arm. The school's head teacher visited my parents and demanded that Mister Chamberlain be put down because he was dangerous. I was heartbroken until my mother came up with a brilliant idea. We gave Mister Chamberlain to the New Zealander, who needed a guard dog at the beach because the bar had been broken into several times. My mother told the head teacher he'd been put down, and that was that.

It was on Ibiza, in the Old Town's harbour, that I saw my first dead man. He had drowned and was floating in the water. I recognized him from the medals still pinned to his jacket as the same old soldier I'd seen drinking in the town's bars. I remember looking down at his body knocking gently against a tied-up fishing boat when another elderly man stopped alongside me and explained that the old man had been in 'la guerra' (the war), that he was 'malo' (bad) and that he'd had it coming for more than 20 years. He told me the old man had seen so much death and destruction that he'd turned to drink to kill the pain. Then one day he fell into the harbour so drunk he couldn't get out. When I asked the old man what side he'd fought for, he told me it didn't matter.

* * *

One day, I was with Mister Chamberlain on the secret beach where he now resided when he galloped off up the rocks behind the beach bar, so I gave chase and eventually he led me to the abandoned village that the New Zealander had bought from the Guardia Civil, who'd taken it over during the civil war.

I heard the dog barking loudly and then spotted him in the distance running inside the village's crumbling church, so I walked through the overgrown square and went after him to investigate. I noticed a side building attached to one end of the church with prison bars at one end.

As I peered through the bars, I could see wooden boxes stacked high up against the back wall of the cell. Some of them had the skull and crossbones sign stamped in red on the side of them indicating arms and explosives, but I was too young to know what that meant at the time.

I was about to leave when Mister Chamberlain began barking from inside the main church building. I walked in to find him sniffing in the corner behind some pews. When I got closer, I noticed smears of blood on the wall, which he was trying to lick. Above them were rusting handcuffs attached by chains to rings in the wall. I also saw a bunch of initials scratched into the wall and realized that people must have been chained up in this corner of the church. I suddenly felt very unsafe, so I walked out.

Mister Chamberlain then dragged me into a cobweb-infested bar next door that looked as if the inhabitants had left in a hurry. Half-full glasses of beer and cognac remained on the bar itself. Dusty bottles of wine were stacked on shelves behind it. In a corner were what looked like boxes of cigarettes and crates of spirits.

Then the dog started barking and began leaping up underneath a couple of huge rotten looking old legs of *jamon* hanging from the ceiling. Suddenly, though, he stopped jumping and turned and bounded off towards the entrance to the bar panting heavily. That was when I noticed a figure standing in the doorway, backlit with the blue sky behind him.

It was the New Zealander owner of the beach. He smiled as he walked in, took down one of the legs of ham, wiped a knife he found in a drawer and sliced a couple of pieces of meat from it. When I looked a bit resistant to eating it, he told me that he kept the meat there because it was cool and that it was now more tasty than it would have been back during the civil war.

I'd thought he'd be annoyed I was snooping around his village, but he just laughed and said he wasn't surprised I was there because I was just like my mother, whose curiosity had nearly cost her her life many times. The New Zealander asked me in a very grown-up way not to tell anyone about what I'd seen in the village. I liked the way he trusted me not to talk about it.

It was one of the first times that I realized there was a dark side to this island life.

CHAPTER THREE
BULLFIGHTING

General Franco's influence was everywhere in the world I inhabited at that time. This was particularly hard for my mother to deal with. Whenever a Guardia Civil officer stopped us in the street and asked for our passports because we were foreigners, I'd notice her staring at their strange triangular hats. They were called Tricornio – which in Spanish means a hat with three sides – and were made out of shiny plastic or vinyl which the sun reflected off in a sinister fashion.

I remember one Guardia Civil officer flicking backwards and forwards through my mother's passport asking why our county was called "The United Kingdom" if our monarch was a queen. He kept saying over and over "Queendom". When my mother refused to engage with him about it, he asked her if something was wrong. I then had to explain in Spanish that her leg was causing her immense pain. She preferred it if I spoke to them, although she spoke fluent Spanish. And you could tell from the expression on the guards' faces that they didn't care about my mother or her missing leg.

Some of the older Guardia Civil officers on Ibiza at that time knew all about my mother's activities during the civil war, though, because they had actually fought in it. And when they inspected our passports, it would be even more tense. They'd also often spit on the ground next to her before turning and walking away. I remember some of them muttering under their breath "puta de una pierna" (one-legged whore).

Ibiza's original residents back then included many hard-faced women of all ages dressed entirely in black, who stared at all the foreigners with suspicious, narrowing eyes. They'd regularly be sitting on benches in plazas (squares) that often featured a statue of General Franco to remind citizens who was in charge.

One time when I was about eight, my mother collected me from the local school wearing an almost see-through dress over a bikini. I knew it would upset the black-clad local mothers, so I grabbed her hand tight and virtually pulled her out of the playground. As we walked up the dusty street away from the school, I noticed one of the older women in black watching us and then getting up and starting to walk in our direction. My mother ignored her. The tight-faced woman caught up with us and, as my mother turned around, spat right in her face.

My mother continued ignoring the woman, which provoked her to try and kick the shin of my mother's one good leg. The woman missed and fell over herself. Instead of humiliating her, my mother just held her head up high, and we walked on.

It wasn't that surprising my mother was loathed by many of the locals. She'd fought on the losing side during the civil war, and when it came to that conflict, memories remained long and bitter.

No doubt that was why the head teacher sent my mother a note saying they wanted me to leave the school because my poor Spanish was holding up all the other pupils in my class. It was just a feeble excuse to get the "son of the whore" out of their precious school.

* * *

The civil war seemed to loom over virtually everything that happened to me when I was young. After leaving that local school, my mother decided I should be educated at the commune run by her old International Brigades friend and former US Army sniper known to everyone as American Joe.

He was a spindly man in his late fifties who wore little else but a skimpy pair of swimming trunks and Ibiza's obligatory flip-flops. He had the first ponytail on a man I ever remember seeing. American Joe had an intense expression on his face, even when he was sucking on a joint. He seemed to have three German girlfriends living with him at the commune, which consisted of half a dozen ramshackle old farm buildings about two miles behind the secret beach. But none of this bothered me, because characters like American Joe had become part of the fabric of my life by this time. I didn't notice they were very different from most other people.

I was much happier being schooled at the commune, mainly because there were only two other kids in my class and we didn't do much except strum on a guitar and talk about the importance of peace throughout the world. Two of American Joe's German girlfriends were our teachers. They spoke excellent English and one of them was particularly nice to me. She had a kind face and always took the time to explain stuff to me.

The commune was supposed to represent all the newly initiated Swinging Sixties elements, from free love to co-operative living, but most of the people American Joe had living there seemed to be mainly rundown drunks, who'd absconded from their home countries. It was only later I discovered that most of them were off their heads on LSD and magic mushrooms most of the time, which explained why they drifted around the commune in such a spaced-out state.

I felt comfortable at the commune. It was like a cosy enclave where I could avoid getting pulled into my parents' disputes and heavy drinking.

* * *

From about the age of eight, my father began taking me to bullfights, very much against the wishes of my mother, who said she thought it was a barbaric practice. He assured her that watching them would be good for me, but all he really wanted was an excuse to gamble.

Ibiza's one and only bullring was also regularly used for gatherings of Franco's pro-nationalist supporters at that time. They considered bullfighting an important example of traditional old style Spanish values. During the civil war, the communists had pledged to ban all such activities, so there was an element of defiance about bullfighting, as far as old school fascists were concerned. The bullring itself had been built in the late 1920s, well before the civil war, and by the 1960s, it had definitely seen better times.

On my very first visit to it, I asked my father why my mother was so upset about us going, as we sat down in our seats in the auditorium among a crowd of a couple of thousand noisy locals. He ignored my question, and something told me not to ask him again, but I do remember deciding there and then that I'd have to find out the answer to that question myself sooner or later.

I'd already heard rumours about shootings taking place in the bullring during the civil war, though no one seemed comfortable saying exactly what had happened. I later learned that one of the Guardia Civil officers my father chatted to at the bullring had been in a unit of officers who patrolled on horseback around the island throughout the civil war.

* * *

Despite all the contrasting beliefs that came out of the civil war, the locals didn't consider the winners and losers in simple black and white terms. It seemed that each side begrudgingly respected the other's commitment to the cause and acknowledged that they had both genuinely believed they had Spanish interests at heart.

But when it came to the foreigners who'd fought with the International Brigades, there remained much anger and bitterness. I remember my mother being lectured by one local fisherman when we were on the boat to the secret beach. He explained to her that many on the island had been dragged into the war against their will, but that when it became clear that Franco was going to win, most simply went with the flow and changed sides to support him virtually overnight. It was all in the name of survival.

That same fisherman told my mother that the International Brigades 'foreigners' were seen as nothing more than spoilt, bored young people from rich countries, who turned to communism without a thought for the consequences of their actions and then travelled to Spain for an adventure.

The New Zealander who owned the secret beach eventually decided that the barriers between International Brigades members and the locals needed to be torn down. After all, it was the 1960s now, and it had been more than two decades since the civil war. So the New Zealander turned his ramshackle beach bar into neutral territory for both sides of the conflict. He genuinely felt it was time for everyone to put all their differences behind them.

He started going out of his way to encourage certain fascists and other locals to come, although initially most of them ended up glaring at the foreigners across the bar much of the time. At first, my mother and her civil war friends tended to try and avoid the bar whenever any of their "enemies" were there. The New Zealander – to his credit – kept reminding them all about how they should learn to live and let live.

Eventually, some Guardia Civil officers began turning up there after mooring their green and white patrol boats at the beach's rickety wooden jetty. They'd leave their black triangular hats on the bar while they supped beers, coffees and cognacs, often provided free by the New Zealander. The sight of those hats still sent a shiver up my mother's spine and those of many of the other International Brigades vets. But gradually a kind of peace treaty between them all was achieved, and everyone ended up using the bar together.

Around the same time, some rich Americans began turning up on the secret beach. These included one old-time Hollywood actor, who'd actually fought with the International Brigades alongside my mother. My father, as a former journalist, convinced this actor to allow him to ghostwrite his memoirs. He hadn't earned a penny out of newspapers since being fired all those years earlier, so this was hopefully going to be great for our family.

Initially, the actor and my father got on very well. One night, the actor even stayed at our villa while they went through the material to put in a book proposal, which my father was going to present to a publisher in London. I overheard them talking about the huge advance they thought they'd get.

But the following day, my mother and the actor were up earlier than my father and headed to the secret beach with me. A few hours later, my badly hungover father finally arrived there by boat, only to discover my mother's back being smeared in coconut oil by the Hollywood actor. I remember he stopped and stood about 20 yards from them before turning round and heading straight to the beach bar. I later found out he'd decided not to confront them because he was hoping to make a big fee out of writing the actor's autobiography. Money that we all badly needed.

However, later that morning, the actor got drunk at the beach bar, professed his undying love for my mother and called my father "a fucking parasite" before grabbing a bottle off the bar and throwing it at him. It missed, but the New Zealander stepped in and prevented them having a full-on fight, and ordered the actor to get the next boat back to the village. As he left, he screamed at my father that the book deal was dead in the water. My father then turned on my mother and accused her of costing him a fortune. She ignored him and ordered another sangria laced with gin at the bar.

The actor committed suicide a few weeks later in Los Angeles. After my mother read about it in a newspaper at the villa one morning, she was plunged into a dark depression, which upset my father because it was so blatantly obvious she was heartbroken.

Eventually my father got himself another supposedly lucrative book deal. He refused to tell us what it was about, but at least the commission seemed to improve his mood. We left him in the villa most mornings to get on with writing and went off to the secret beach. Throughout the writing process, my father wouldn't let us look at any drafts of the book, claiming that would be a bad omen.

About a week before the book was due to be published, a box full of printed and bound copies of the hardback arrived at the main post office in the Old Town. My mother and I went to pick it up, while my father slept off yet another hangover. At the post office, my mother ripped open the package and took out a copy, looked at the cover and froze. It was the same Hollywood actor's autobiography. She took me to a nearby bar, ordered a stiff drink and sat down to read the book.

Back at home that evening, my father was confronted by my mother. He claimed he'd interviewed the actor before he left the island. My mother accused him of making it all up, including a section about the actor's experiences during the civil war, which were all identical to what she'd told my father long before.

"Why do you care so much?" he said to my mother. "I got a big advance and we need the money."

She was so furious with my father, she stormed out of the villa with me that same evening and we went to live at American Joe's commune, where I was already attending school. After the book's publication, my father was shunned by all my mother's civil war friends, many of whom were regulars at the New Zealander's beach bar.

After my mother had left, my father began drowning himself in booze and living the life of a hermit in the home where we'd once all resided happily together. As a result of his absence, the wily old New Zealander became something of a father figure to me at that time. He'd often sit down with me and spill a few secrets from the island's civil war past.

One time, he told me how Hitler's Luftwaffe had been called in by Franco to strafe hundreds of evacuees as they walked along the island's only main road from the town of San Antonio to the capital, Ibiza Old Town. Franco did this because he wanted to strike fear into his citizens in order to make sure they didn't rise up against him or talk openly about any of the atrocities committed on the island. And Hitler had wanted to test out some of his most lethal war machines before the impending Second World War, so lent Franco the tools for the job.

The corpses of the dozens of locals killed that day were left to rot on the highway, as the Guardia Civil threatened to shoot anyone who tried to give them a proper burial.

* * *

When I was almost 12, my uncle turned up on one of his infrequent visits to Ibiza and stayed with us at the villa, which we'd moved back into after my father decided to live in London following the split with my mother. My uncle seemed very concerned by my schooling at the commune.

All I knew about my uncle at this time was that he lived in London, but no one ever said what he did for a job. My father usually ignored my mother whenever she mentioned him, so I didn't feel able to ask them much about him. But he always bought me a toy when he visited from London, so he seemed brilliant to me.

American Joe and my uncle knew each other from the civil war, but there was no love lost between them and my uncle warned my mother to steer well clear of him. He said I should be taken out of the commune school and given a "proper fucking education" in the UK.

I was desperate not to leave Ibiza, though. When my mother tried to reason with my uncle to change his mind, he pointed out that she was a very special person but that parenting was not one of her finest skills. Even she had to smile at that remark. Looking back on it now, my uncle clearly only wanted what was best for me.

Whatever he said, my mother always seemed to end up agreeing with it, anyway, so I was packed off to a boarding school in the home counties, south of London. I knew I'd hate every minute of it, but there was no point in confronting her or any of the other so-called adults.

I only found out after I got there that the school was run by solemn, strict and humourless Catholic priests. It turned out that the headmaster's brother knew my uncle and that it was the only school that would take me at such short notice, having not had a proper English education, without sitting an entrance exam.

I'd never been to church in my entire life, and the only Catholics I'd ever seen were Ibiza's women in black, most of whom seemed to loathe everyone in sight. Worse still, I spoke English with a Spanish/German accent at this time, which provoked a lot of face-pulling and nasty xenophobic comments from pupils and teachers alike.

Three weeks after I began at the school, my uncle turned up in a British racing green Jaguar X-Type sports car with spoked wheels. He was smoking a big fat cigar and had a beautiful girlfriend by his side. He told me he'd come to see me to "try and keep my spirits up". I begged him to let me leave the school and return to Ibiza immediately. He laughed and patted me on the head and said I should trust him because it would all be worth it in the end.

My uncle often picked me up and took me out for scrumptious cream teas, which soon became the highlight of my life at the school. He'd always arrive there at the wheel of a different car, usually with a girlfriend in tow. My uncle seemed an even more colourful character than he'd been in Ibiza, with his snazzy pinstripe suits and initialled cufflinks, rounded off with a dandy silk polka-dot bowtie. He talked about "cash jobs" and "ducking and diving" all the time, so it was clear that he didn't have a normal 9–5 job.

But he never spoke to me about my mother and father. I remember asking him once what my mother had been like as a child, and he completely ignored the question. I overheard him in his car telling one girlfriend he wasn't "too impressed" with my mother and father as parents and that was why he'd felt obliged to "look after me". But he did get very angry when that girlfriend described my mother as "an old tart", so clearly there was some loyalty there.

My uncle and I were out having yet another cream tea one day when he slipped out of the teashop to make a call from a nearby phone box. Moments later, he came rushing back in and insisted we had to go to London urgently. When I mentioned that my school was expecting me back soon, he

assured me that he'd call them and that they would understand if I was dropped off a bit later than usual.

Within an hour, we were cruising through Notting Hill in
West London in his latest sports car. Back in those days, it was
a vast slum area – a complete contrast to what it has become
today. My uncle eventually stopped outside a tall, dilapidated
stucco-fronted house. A man came out with an envelope,
which he handed through the open car window to my uncle.
After that, we sped off.

At the next crumbling property, my uncle had a nasty
row with a one-eyed man in the house's front garden, which
was full of rotting old mattresses. When he got back in the
car, I asked him who the man was. He laughed and ruffled
me on the head like he always did when I asked any awkward
questions.

Then, while pulling out of a parking space, he almost
crashed into another vehicle he hadn't seen. The other driver
gave him a "V" sign and my uncle swung the car round and
began chasing the other one maniacally through the narrow
streets. At the next set of red traffic lights, my uncle got out,
marched up to the other car and pulled the driver out. Then
he punched him in the face before calmly walking back to his
car and driving off without another word.

It wasn't the time or the place to ask him any more questions.

* * *

My uncle paid for me to get a *Daily Mirror* delivered every morning to my dormitory at school. As had been the case on Ibiza, a newspaper provided me with more useful information than anything I studied in the classroom. But my *Daily Mirror* delivery made me even more unpopular with staff and pupils, as they all looked down on it as a "common tabloid rag". This snobbery was not the only reason I was picked on, though. Racist and antisemitic nicknames were two a penny at my typical British school, and one of my classmates nicknamed me "the yid" because of my long nose. I learned to take that sort of stuff with a pinch of salt.

One evening, I was walking up a corridor towards my dormitory when I saw one of my class's worst bullies holding the school's only black pupil up against a wall and calling him a "rich darkie" while he searched through his pockets for cash to steal. I pulled the bully off the boy, fully expecting a kicking for my troubles, but instead the boy and I immediately teamed up together and gave that racist a bloody nose.

As we were exiting the scene of the crime, we walked straight into our house master. He could clearly see what had happened, but the bully was too proud to accuse us of anything, so we were allowed to go unpunished. More importantly, that African boy went on to become my best and only real friend at that school.

* * *

I went back to Ibiza every school holiday. Back there, my mother had begun partying even harder than when she'd been with my father, and I started to find it quite awkward to be on the island. Ibiza was now feeling a bit strange to me. I didn't seem to fit in like I had when I was younger.

My mother had become friendly with a German man who talked openly about being a member of the Baader-Meinhof terror cell. By this time, nothing surprised me about my mother. It was the late 1960s and Ibiza seemed to be evolving into a free love, hippy version of Vienna back in the 1930s. The island attracted an eclectic mix of people, but there were also some very shady characters there. I remember my mother's German friend talking to someone at the beach bar about how agents from Israel's spy service Mossad had turned up disguised as hippies in order to monitor members of the Baader-Meinhof group, who'd by that time joined forces with the Palestinian Liberation Organization led by Yasser Arafat.

* * *

About a year after I started at that boarding school in the home counties, my mother sent me a letter saying that she and my father had reconciled and that they couldn't wait for me to get back to the island for the holidays. I was surprised they'd got back together, because my mother had been so upset by that fake autobiography my father had written. But on the other hand, my mother was a very forgiving person in many ways, so, looking back on it, I guess it was kind of inevitable.

Flying to and from Ibiza was not as easy as it is today. I had to change planes in Barcelona, Valencia or Palma, Mallorca, and then catch a smaller, older plane to and from the island. On the journey out from London after my parent's reconciliation, I found myself on a rattling old Dakota twin-engine propellor aircraft, originally built in wartime, sitting next to an old lady in black with a live chicken on her lap. As we approached Ibiza's tiny airport, there was a huge bang and one of the engines burst into flames.

The propellor blade immediately buckled and the Dakota began dipping alarmingly. Below us those rice fields near the secret beach were getting closer by the second. The Dakota eventually levelled out at about 500 feet, and a few seconds later the undercarriage went down with a loud clump and the wheels crunched into the mud as we did an emergency landing.

It took the fire brigade and hated Guardia Civil at least 20 minutes to reach us. The Guardia Civil eventually led us all out of the plane's emergency exit and onto the waterlogged field, where we squelched through the shallow marshlands towards half a dozen flatbed trucks parked in the distance. As I was walking over, I noticed one of the older Guardia Civil officers – whom I'd seen a few times at the New Zealander's beach bar – smiling knowingly at me as I walked past him. When he asked after my mother, I didn't answer.

CHAPTER FOUR
THE MTB

Following that Dakota crash, I refused to fly anymore. Also, the island began feeling even more like a very backward, isolated place compared to London. My parents were constantly arguing despite their recent reconciliation, so I made it clear to my mother I'd rather be in London during the school holidays. My uncle then thankfully stepped in and said I could stay on an old wartime Motor Torpedo Boat (MTB) that he'd converted into his home and kept moored on the River Thames in Chelsea, West London. My father's only response was to question why my uncle would buy a boat when he couldn't even swim. My mother replied how she always did, which was that it was a free world and my uncle could do whatever he wanted.

He'd bought the naval boat "for a song" from a Thameside scrap yard a few years earlier. He told me he liked it because he could move it up and down the river whenever he needed to "keep a low profile", as he put it. A low profile from what, I didn't know. Sometimes, at low tide on the Thames, the boat would end up sitting on a bed of wine, beer and spirit bottles which had been drunkenly chucked overboard by my uncle and his associates.

The rusting vessel was still painted wartime grey, so it looked a bit rough from the outside, but inside it was filled to the brim with expensive antique furniture and his favourite jazz music (similar taste to my mother's), and this made it feel more like a floating gin palace than a former wartime gunboat.

My uncle loved music. One day, after hearing how much I'd played over in Ibiza, he bought me a guitar, and during the hotter summer months, he'd hook up three speakers on the MTB's deck for his music. This infuriated many of his wealthy neighbours in some of the big houses overlooking the river.

As well as ensuring he had great music at all times, my uncle was also obsessed with security on his MTB. He kept a big safe hidden in a wardrobe, which is probably why he didn't like anyone going into the hull below our living quarters. One time when he was out doing his "collections", I sneaked down to take a peek and discovered that the main section of the hull was sealed by a locked metal door with a huge handle. I was intrigued by what I'd found but didn't dare ask my uncle what was behind the door.

Upstairs in the MTB's sitting room area was a photo on a sideboard of my uncle during the 1930s with three friends in pinstripe suits looking menacingly at a bunch of Oswald Mosley's notorious Black Shirt fascists marching past them in the East End of London. I only know these details because I asked him about the photo, but I did also recognize one of the men in the photo from articles I'd read in the *Daily Mirror* delivered to me at school. He'd been nicknamed in the press "The Crime King of London" and often featured in newspaper exposés about the notorious Soho underworld.

Little about my uncle surprised me by that time. Heavy-set men in dark suits would turn up in the early hours with heavy boxes they'd take down to the secret compartment in the MTB's hull. Similar-looking characters would later arrive to pick up the same stuff. My uncle knew he didn't need to order me to keep quiet about whatever I saw and heard on that boat, as I already knew not to tell anyone.

At school, I started cutting out and keeping articles about some of the criminal types I began encountering with my uncle in London. I'd stick those cuttings in a scrapbook I kept hidden under my bed in the dormitory. The majority of my time at school was spent longing for the holidays because that meant freedom and life in the real world, as opposed to the controlled environment of a boarding school.

My best and only friend remained my school's only black pupil, and we often discussed running away because it felt like the school was doing nothing but cramping our style. We both thought we were ready to take on the world. We even convinced ourselves we didn't need an education. During the holidays, I sometimes stayed at his family's enormous mansion on Wimbledon Common. His father was the UK ambassador for the newly independent Democratic Republic of West Africa (DRWA). We had the run of the house because his parents were often attending cocktail parties and diplomatic events. I was delighted not to be anywhere near Ibiza at the time.

Back on the MTB, my uncle insisted I had to earn my keep if I was going to stay with him for long periods of time during my school holidays and told me he had a job for me. We'd go off in his latest car to carry out his "collections" from dozens of rundown rental properties, mainly in the Notting Hill slums. He taught me how to drive his car, so that I could sit behind the wheel with the engine running in case we had to make a fast getaway.

One time – when I was about 16 – my uncle took me up to a Soho drinking club where the same notorious Crime King of London I'd earlier come across with him was hosting a launch party for his much-anticipated autobiography. Many of the gangsters were in obligatory three-piece double-fronted pinstripe suits that made them look like Chicago gangsters from the 1930s. There were also a few actors and a couple of minor members of the royal family at the party. I loved it there because the guests all treated me as if I was an adult.

Two men I met there spent ages talking to me. I remember one was called "Smelly", which seemed a pretty tame nickname compared to what I was used to at boarding school. I never discovered the other man's name, but I was intrigued by him because he didn't look like all the other criminals I'd met with my uncle in London. He was skinny, had a middle-class English accent and wore wire-rimmed specs that made him look like a college professor.

About halfway through the party, my uncle insisted on talking to Smelly and the other man out of earshot from me. I watched closely as my uncle gritted his teeth and got very irritated with the two other men as they talked intensely. They were arguing about some money owed to my uncle. When Smelly and the other criminal with the wire-rimmed glasses started talking to the Crime King in another corner of the bar, my uncle and I left the book launch. He seemed angry about something.

Just before we parked up near his MTB, I plucked up the courage to ask him what was wrong, as he hadn't said a word all the way back. He snapped back that it was none of my "fucking business". Then he thought better of it and tried to make a joke of it all by ruffling my hair and laughing.

A few days later, I went back to boarding school for the new term and my uncle suddenly stopped coming to take me out on Saturday afternoons. He never wrote or called to explain why. I thought it was because he was angry with me for asking awkward questions about that Soho book launch.

On my uncle's birthday a few weeks later, I called my mother in Ibiza and used it as an excuse to ask her where he'd gone. She sounded strange and detached on the phone – even by her standards – and insisted that she didn't know where my uncle was and that I should study hard at school and forget about him. When I insisted she tell me what was going on, she put the phone down.

A couple of weeks after that, my mother turned up at my school in a rental car and took me off for the weekend. She'd convinced the headmaster that I needed compassionate leave. I knew it had to be connected to my uncle, but she refused to answer my questions on the drive into London and we ended up hardly exchanging a word.

Then we arrived at my uncle's MTB moored in Chelsea, I thought it might all be some kind of belated surprise for his birthday. But when I saw that the front door to the main cabin was wide open and flapping in the breeze, I turned to my mother and knew something was wrong. She'd gone very pale and stopped on the deck at the end of the gangplank onto the boat, until I grabbed her arm and we stepped gingerly into the main cabin.

The first thing I noticed was that 1930s photo of my uncle watching the Blackshirts at the fascist rally in the East End was lying face upwards with the glass cracked. Then I saw two armchairs overturned nearby. The rest of the interior looked like a bomb had hit it. Everything had been turned upside down. Tables, chairs, even the sofa. In the kitchen, glasses and plates lay smashed and sprawled across the floor. Someone had clearly been looking for something very important.

My mother stopped in the middle of the main cabin, pulled a packet of cigarettes out of her handbag and lit one with a shaking hand. Then she stepped carefully over the broken glass to the bar in the corner. All the tumblers on the shelves behind it had been smashed, but she leaned down beneath the counter and produced a three-quarters-empty bottle of whisky, untwisted the lid and took a long swig directly from it. Then she threw her cigarette out of an open porthole and announced we had work to do.

We spent hours cleaning up the inside of the MTB. My mother wouldn't discuss where my uncle was. I told her I needed to find a mop and sneaked down to the hull to see if that big metal door had been broken open. My uncle had pushed a huge cupboard in front of it since I'd last been on the boat, and the raiders didn't seem to have discovered it.

After asking my mother for at least the tenth time where my uncle was, she slumped in a chair in floods of tears and said, "He's gone. He's gone", over and over again. I presumed that meant he was dead, but my mother refused to elaborate any further.

That night, we stayed on the boat. I was kept awake by the sound of my mother's nonstop sobbing from my uncle's bedroom next to me. On at least two occasions during the night, I went in and tried to console her. But as soon as I would come round to asking her about my uncle, she'd order me out of the bedroom.

The following morning, she announced we were going to a pub in south London to meet a couple of my uncle's closest associates. She said that everything would become much clearer after she met with them.

On arrival at the pub, she left me in the car and entered the premises. Moments later, two of my uncle's Soho friends arrived in a white American Cadillac convertible I'd seen parked outside the book launch the previous month.

Two hours later, my mother staggered out of the pub tipsily clutching a brown envelope in her hand. She got in and slapped the unsealed envelope on the dashboard before ordering me to move behind the wheel because she wanted me to drive us home. I noticed a roll of crisp new bank notes held together by an elastic band inside the envelope.

I leaned forward to turn the key to start the car when she grabbed my arm.

"Stop a moment. I've got something to tell you," she said.

Then she tearfully admitted that my uncle was in prison.

"But you mustn't tell your father you know because he didn't want me to tell you."

She never told me what my uncle had done, but at the time it was no big surprise he'd ended up in jail. The most important thing to me was that he wasn't dead.

The following day, my mother and I went to Wandsworth Prison in south London to see my uncle. In the car park, we bumped into one of the same men who'd given my mother that money in the pub the previous day. He winked at us, but no other words were exchanged.

The Victorian-built prison itself was austere, cold and extremely uninviting. The wardens seemed very grumpy and opinionated. I didn't like the way they patted down my mother – who was wearing a mink coat and heels – in a suggestive manner and refused to let her take her walking stick into the main building.

As we were about to enter the refectory area where inmates were waiting for their visitors, my mother – who'd been using me for support – slipped and fell onto the floor. As she grabbed at me to help get her off the floor, she suddenly announced I should go in on my own because she didn't feel very well. Then she slumped down on a bench in the reception area with her hair in disarray and stockings laddered, pulled out a flask and took a long sip.

I knew I had to step up and take over the situation. So I continued on into the refectory area where I saw my uncle sitting at a table, tapping his fingers as if he'd been there for ages waiting for us. He smiled when he saw me, but then his eyes narrowed when he realized my mother wasn't with me.

I sat down nervously at a small table opposite him. He seemed disappointed when I told him she was ill.

But my uncle didn't seem in the least bit fazed by prison, and I soon realized he'd most likely been behind bars before. He nodded at one of the prison officers and then winked at another inmate, who sat down near us with his family. All this made me feel instantly at ease. So I told him all about how his boat had been turned upside down, but reassured him they hadn't found the secret door to the hull. He smiled and said the police had been looking for something they would never find.

By this stage, I wasn't surprised by anything he was telling me, and his demeanour was so relaxed that I wasn't particularly worried about his situation. He insisted he'd soon be released within days because his lawyer was going to nail the police for "fitting him up".

Then his tone hardened and he looked me straight in my eyes.

"Just make sure you look after your mother, alright?"

I nodded, delighted to be given such responsibility. Then he paused and his expression changed. His voice lowered and he told me he didn't want either of us to visit him again in prison and repeated that it was down to me to take care of my mother.

I couldn't understand why he wouldn't want us to visit him again. After all, I saw myself as his confidant, the person he could rely on, and now it felt as if he'd rejected me. He must have seen the hurt in my eyes, but he didn't say another word. So I got up to go. As I walked out of the refectory area, I turned to wave goodbye to him, but he'd already left.

In the car on the way back to my uncle's MTB, my mother went into yet another one of her shell-like moods and didn't say a word.

* * *

My father was waiting on the wooden jetty next to my uncle's MTB when we arrived back from prison that day. My mother urged me not to stop when we saw him, but he spotted us immediately. I'd thought he was in Ibiza.

My parents ended up having a massive row next to the rental car while I was sitting in it. During the argument, I heard my father say that my mother should never have taken me to visit my uncle in prison, whom he described as "a bloody criminal". My father then accused her of loving someone else more than she loved him. My mother yelled back at him that she wished she'd never met him and that she hated his guts.

That was the last straw for my father. He turned and walked away from her, muttering that he never wanted to see her ever again.

CHAPTER FIVE
TIME TO WORK

I returned to Ibiza with my mother when my school holidays began two weeks after her row with my father. I'd made that promise to my uncle in prison to look after her, so I even agreed to travel by plane, despite my fears about flying since that Dakota crash.

But I hadn't really wanted to go back to Ibiza. I refused to go to the New Zealander's beach with my mother because I couldn't face seeing her drunk on virtually a daily basis. Everything I had thought "normal" about my life was suddenly proving much harder to handle.

It even felt like I was turning into my mother's carer. But I didn't want to reject her, because she seemed so fragile a lot of the time, especially after we went to the prison to see my uncle. Inevitably, though, I did gradually start to feel resentful towards my mother. I was becoming more rebellious and unwilling to always be at her beck and call day and night. To her credit, she allowed for the fact I was evolving into a typical, stroppy youth, and eventually asked me if I'd prefer to live in London. I jumped at the chance, naturally.

She said I could stay on my uncle's old MTB on condition I didn't contact my father, who was living quite nearby in London by this time. It was a twisted deal, but I didn't question it because all I cared about was living in London on my own.

* * *

Soon after moving onto my absent uncle's MTB, my best and only friend from school came to stay with me. He seemed very distracted, though, and turned out to be as angry about his life as I was about mine.

I'd just read in a newspaper that there had been a coup in his home country, the DRWA. The report said my best friend's father had been the driving force behind it and was expected to take over as president. He told me that his entire family had travelled back to the DRWA without him after he'd refused to leave London. He'd been cast aside by them, in a sense. No wonder he seemed so angry.

We were very much in the same boat, because my mother had just left me to fend for myself in London, so I let him move into the MTB for the rest of the school holidays. We both looked on London as an escape route from our families, or so we both thought. We'd both just turned 17 but were over 6 feet tall and looked much older, so we became single men instead of schoolboys. We began drinking heavily, taking drugs and sleeping with girls.

I even picked up some new friends in local pubs near where my uncle's MTB was moored in west London and became quite well known locally for holding wild parties on the boat.

* * *

It was the mid-1970s, and Ibiza was becoming awash with drugs. New clubs were opening regularly as increasing numbers of visitors began turning up from all over Europe and beyond. And as the tourist invasion kicked in, the Guardia Civil were out patrolling the streets, keeping an eye on the unconventional, carefree visitors and hippy inhabitants of the island. They seemed prepared to let them do whatever they wanted, as long as they didn't encourage the locals to rise up against them.

But change was in the air. By early 1975, Franco was a sickly old man and Spaniards were actually starting to contemplate a future without him for the first time since he'd won the civil war back in 1939. There were constant updates on Franco's ill health reported almost every day in the Spanish press, and many accepted that his rule was finally close to expiring.

* * *

Back in London, myself and my best friend didn't want to return to school at the end of the holidays. We thought we no longer needed an education, which made us extremely restless and unruly pupils. This wasn't helped by the fact that all our classmates and teachers seemed to disapprove of the way we'd teamed up as friends. I don't know if it was to do with us being black and white or what, but we both felt alienated. Many pupils avoided us, and teachers began going out of their way to try and keep us apart during class time.

Boys would sneer at us in the school corridors, and one time another pupil spat in both our meals in the school refectory and then challenged us to have a go at him. But we didn't fall for the bait, because we were well aware that staff were watching us closely waiting for any excuse to reprimand us.

A few months after my seventeenth birthday, we'd just entered the showers after a game of rugby when three other boys cornered us. They called my friend a nigger and me an oven-dodger, which was yet another antisemitic reference to my large nose.

"We're gonna teach you two a lesson you'll never forget," said the ringleader.

Then two of them pulled out knives and started trying to slash at us both. I smashed one of them over the wrist with my rugby boot so hard that his weapon fell to the floor. My friend managed to twist the other boy's knife out of his hand.

We'd picked up the weapons and were standing brandishing them at our three attackers when a teacher walked in. He thought we'd used the weapons to attack the three bullies. We immediately put the knives down and tried to explain what had happened but were then marched off to see the headmaster, who was a priest.

He threatened to call the police – even after we'd explained what had occurred – and insisted we had to apologize to the bullies. We refused and were locked in an adjoining room, while the headmaster rang my mother, who'd been on a visit to London at the time.

She turned up at the school a couple of hours later and – after we'd explained what had really happened – demanded that the three racist pupils be expelled. The headmaster priest refused and blamed everything on the two of us, saying we were "out of control" and had been causing trouble for months. We were then expelled on the spot.

On the train journey back to London, my mother seemed relieved I was no longer attending the school. "I never wanted you to go there in the first place," she said. She also revealed to me for the first time that I was actually Jewish through her bloodline. This perhaps explained her unusually strong response to the story of the fight.

My Jewish heritage had never been mentioned before. She said she'd kept it secret because admitting to being Jewish had been extremely dangerous during both the the Second World War and the Spanish Civil War. This presented me with an opportunity to find out something more about her wartime experiences. I'd heard stories about atrocities on Ibiza but never directly from her. So I asked her to tell me how she ended up on the island. She hesitated at first, insisting she didn't want to live in the past. I must have looked very disappointed because – despite being clearly uncomfortable about the entire subject – she finally opened up.

She started by explaining how she and my uncle and dozens of other International Brigades soldiers were captured by the fascists on the mainland near Valencia following a defeat during one of the civil war's most brutal ground battles in late 1938. The International Brigades members were chained to each other and taken in a container ship to Ibiza. My mother was only one of two women in a group of at least forty prisoners.

My mother said that Franco's forces considered Ibiza to be far enough away from the prying eyes of the mainland to enable them to do what they wanted with their prisoners, especially the foreigners who'd dared to think they could play a role in Spain's internal conflict.

After docking at Ibiza old port, the prisoners – including my mother and my uncle – had been left on board the ship in the searing heat for more than 24 hours without any food or water. The following day they were all marched five miles in chains to the Ibiza bullring, where they spent a further two days without food and with only a small ration of one cup of water each.

Then a dozen Guardia Civil officers armed with Tommy guns rode into the bullring on horseback.

"They trotted their horses around and around us," explained my mother. "We could hardly breathe for the clouds of dust and all the time they just kept studying us. It went on for half an hour at least. We were terrified."

Those same Guardia Civil officers then took aim with their Tommy guns and shot at least 20 male prisoners. When they'd finished firing, they got off their horses and spat in the faces of every dead prisoner before doing the same to the ones who were still alive, including my mother and uncle. All the remaining prisoners were then marched in chains some miles along a rock-strewn track to a makeshift prison camp, which had been hastily constructed to house the enemies of General Francisco Franco.

"That was it. Our war was over after that," said my mother, as our train slowed down for arrival at Paddington Station.

I didn't get another chance to talk to her about what happened in that camp while we were in London. But at least I'd managed to start unpeeling the extraordinary story of her life.

* * *

The following day we arrived back on Ibiza, and I soon found that having been expelled from school with an incomplete education didn't exactly provide me with a rosy future to look forward to.

I felt very complicated about my parents, too. So when my father turned up on the island just a few days after us, it completely threw me and my mother, especially since he was dating a German woman by this time. It turned out he'd come back to the island to sort out a divorce settlement. But I knew my mother would try to avoid meeting him because she didn't really want a divorce, despite everything that had happened between them. So my mother and father played phone tag with each other, even though they were staying only a few miles apart on the island.

Then one morning, my mother got up much earlier than me and headed off to her favourite beach. I heard her leave and was convinced she'd taken the early boat to try and avoid bumping into my father there. I ended up taking a mid-morning boat to the beach and strode across the burning hot sand towards my mother's favourite sunbathing spot on the secret beach, only to find a strange man smothering coconut oil on her back.

She introduced him to me as a film director from Holly-wood, who was interested in turning her life story into a film. The pair had apparently exchanged letters over the previous six months. I had no idea about this, as she'd never mentioned him before. It turned out he'd first heard about her from that same actor whose autobiography my father invented in order to get a lucrative publishing deal.

This movie director seemed much more enamoured with my mother than she was of him. But then this was often the case when it came to her. She could be open and flirty with men and women one minute and then cruelly blank to them the next. It was all a game to her.

I listened to my mother explaining to her new Hollywood friend that the main reason she hated having lost her leg was that people tried to use it as an excuse to pry into her private life. I'd heard her say the same thing many times before, so there was a definite element of truth about it.

On the beach that day, though, she switched the conversation with the Hollywood director to my father and talked about him as if they were still together. She insisted to the director that she'd fallen in love with my father because he hadn't mentioned her missing leg when they first met.

I stayed on the beach next to them that day listening to their conversation, which included him asking her if she'd ever killed someone in battle during the civil war. Instead of answering, she giggled girlishly and told him to make sure he covered every inch of her back with that coconut oil and then reminded him in a flirtatious voice that she was still waiting for him to give her the written outline of the movie he was hoping to make about her life.

He apologized profusely and took a carefully bound document out of his beach bag and passed it to her sheepishly. I suggested we go to the beach bar to give my mother time to read through the outline. We ended up on a corner table in the bar with a couple of ice-cold cervezas, and I worked the conversation round to my mother (which wasn't hard) and asked him if she'd told him how she lost her leg, without admitting she'd never told me. He seemed a bit taken aback at first, so I rephrased the question to make it sound like I was just checking that he had the facts right in his story outline.

He said it had happened while my mother and uncle were being held in the prison camp on Ibiza. They suspected that the fascists planned to execute all the prisoners who'd survived the bullring massacre, including both of them. So they hatched a plan to escape, which involved cutting a hole in the camp's wire perimeter fence in the dead of night. They managed to get out and headed for the nearby coastline with the intention of following it to a small nearby port. Eventually they found themselves scrambling along a cliff edge, from which my uncle fell into the sea. My mother dived in to rescue him because he couldn't swim. My mother managed to grab hold of my uncle and had just found a piece of driftwood for him to cling to, when a Guardia Civil patrol boat appeared out in the distance.

As the vessel passed them, its wash swept her away from my uncle. She wasn't worried because she was a strong swimmer, but then the patrol boat did a U-turn and headed back towards them at high speed. She dived under the water, but her leg got caught by the patrol boat's propeller as it passed just above her.

Despite the injury, she and my uncle managed to get back onto dry land and eventually made it to the mainland on a boat stolen from a nearby quayside. But she'd lost a lot of blood. My uncle ended up carrying her to a hospital before running off. The staff at the hospital on the outskirts of Valencia hid her from the fascists because she was a woman and they were Republican sympathizers.

Doctors didn't manage to save her leg, and by the time she got out of the hospital, my uncle had disappeared. She later heard he'd been caught by Franco's forces while trying to secretly cross the Pyrenees mountains between northern Spain and then-neutral France.

Back at the beach bar, the director suddenly stopped telling me all this because my mother was walking towards us. She sat down next to the director and immediately said she didn't want to do the film of her life after all, because it was too painful for her. In any case, she was sure my uncle wouldn't approve, as he was "a very private person" and he was the other "star" of the story. She didn't mention he was in prison. She also told the director she wanted to keep the outline just in case he was ever tempted to make the film without her approval.

* * *

Out in the bay in front of the secret beach – despite the scorching hot sun that morning – a squall had begun rippling across the surface of the sea. Ominously dark clouds also loomed in the distance.

I eventually left my mother talking to the director and went for a walk on the rocks overlooking the beach. I found myself regressing back to being a child by searching for crabs while I tried to compute all the issues thrown up by what the director had just told me.

A few minutes later, I looked down from the rocks and noticed my mother standing waist-high in the sea with a younger woman in a wetsuit holding her as she awkwardly and slightly drunkenly put a water ski on her foot and almost fell into the water as she did it. I had no doubt she'd got so irritated by the pushy Hollywood director that she'd decided to avoid all his questions by taking her first ever water skiing lesson, which with one leg was quite a challenge.

The young German woman who was her instructor held her from behind to make sure she had the ski at the right angle, pointing upwards in the water. When she was properly balanced, the instructor told her to grab onto a rope attached to a speed boat, which was waiting with its engine idling 20 yards ahead of them. My mother tried two or three times to get up on her one ski as the speed boat pulled ahead. But each time she lost her balance and fell backwards into the sea. The speed boat then had to circle round and return to its original position.

Out in the bay, one of the fishing boats that came to the beach every morning was chugging through the choppy waters towards the rundown wooden jetty, overloaded with boxes and crates to be delivered to the beach bar. Down in the shallow water below, the speed boat surged forward and the rope pulling my mother out of the water tightened. This time, she rose majestically on one ski. A bunch of regulars applauded loudly and cheered as they stood watching her from the edge of the beach, including the Hollywood movie director.

Typically, my mother turned and managed a majestic wave in their direction. Moments later, though, the rope crossed the bow of the fishing boat just as it was arriving at the jetty. She lost her balance, but the ski remained attached to her foot and began dragging her towards the fishing boat. Everyone watching from the beach immediately waded into the water as she smashed into the side of the boat so hard that her body seemed to bounce off the hull and she flopped face-down into the water.

I rushed down to the beach from where I'd been on the rocks as the New Zealander and others frantically waded out towards my mother, who was still floating face-down on the surface of the water. The instructor reached her first and expertly dragged her limp body up onto the beach, where she gave her mouth-to-mouth as she lay on her back. I got there just as my mother's emerald eyes snapped open, much to everyone's relief. Without a beat, she sat up as if nothing had happened and thanked the younger woman profusely.

Within half an hour my mother and her rescuer were knocking back her favourite sangrias laced with gin at the bar as the Hollywood director tried his hardest to keep up with them. Every now and again my mother would shout drunkenly in German across at the barman to get them another drink.

Meanwhile, the New Zealander put on a white apron and began poking in a wood-burning fire pit in the corner of the bar before throwing bucket-loads of rice laced with yellow saffron into a huge black pan containing bluey-grey mussels, pink squid, rabbit meat and an assortment of fish in a sea of bright red chilli oil and green peas.

Myself, my mother, her new German lady friend and the Hollywood director eventually sat down at a long table just as my father and his girlfriend walked into the bar and headed for the other end of the same table. I hadn't realized they were even on the beach. It was the first time my mother and father had seen each other since they'd split up in London. Typically, my mother avoided looking directly at him and made a point of touching the Hollywood director's arm as she intensely explained yet again why she didn't want a movie made of her life.

The wine soon began flowing and the New Zealander started serving huge helpings of paella with a massive spatula from that pan sizzling noisily on the open wood fire. I'd just begun strumming on my guitar a few minutes later when I heard the distinct throbbing sound of powerful diesel engines out in the bay. I looked up and saw a bright yellow boat skirting the crests of increasingly large waves as it glided gracefully towards the old wooden jetty.

As the vessel got closer, I noticed enormous, colourful flowers childishly painted on the yellow hull, making it look even more bizarre. It was then I spotted gun turrets on the deck, which looked strangely out of place on a boat painted yellow and covered in huge flowers.

CHAPTER SIX
THE HIPPY BOAT

Next to me, my mother unshackled herself from the director and the German woman and stood up. Then, with her hand across her forehead to keep the bright sunlight out of her eyes, she studied the boat closely.

"Jesus. It's him," she said.

It was only then I realized it was my uncle's MTB.

Standing by the table, the New Zealand owner of the secret beach began laughing out loud and slapping his thighs with the palms of his hand.

"Come on," he shouted at us. "The old bastard's back."

The three of us weaved through the bar and headed down towards the beach. Out in the bay, the MTB was about to reach the jetty.

* * *

A few minutes later, half a dozen of us were crowded round the wooden jetty as my uncle stepped off the gangplank and straight into my mother's arms. I stood alongside them both and he turned to ruffle my hair, just like he'd always done throughout my childhood, only to find I now had a ponytail.

"What the fuck is this?" he said, playfully pulling on it.

I was intrigued by the way he and his friends were so casually dressed compared to how they'd always been in London. I asked him how come he was out of prison, and he grabbed my ponytail again and said: "They couldn't pin anything on me, son."

My uncle, followed by his two crew mates – a 7-foot tall man called "Shorty" and "Smelly" from the book launch – led us off the jetty onto the beach as if he was the pied piper of Ibiza. At the beach bar, they each downed a bottle of San Miguel in two thirst-quenching gulps before grabbing fresh bottles of beer, which they took with them to sit down at the long table next to the big black pan of sizzling paella. My father and his girlfriend were seated, isolated, at the other end.

My uncle greeted almost everyone apart from my father that day as if they were long-lost friends. He even kissed the grumpy little old lady in black who sat knitting outside the toilets. Back at the long table, my father was glaring in our direction as my uncle applauded loudly when I started strumming a song on the guitar. Watching my father closely, I realized he hadn't just come to Ibiza from London to divorce my mother but also because he knew my uncle was out of prison and heading this way.

A few minutes later I returned from the toilet to find that my uncle had left the long table. I looked around and spotted him on the beach in front of the bar deep in conversation with the New Zealander. They seemed to be arguing about something. The New Zealander eventually turned and walked away from my uncle, who was shouting something after him and wagging his finger. I remember looking across at my mother, who was still seated at the long table, but she was watching them both so avidly she didn't notice me.

* * *

Just after my uncle sat down again at the table, my mother's American director friend asked him why he was in Ibiza.

"Just popped over to see a few old friends," said my uncle. "Then I've gotta get down to Tangiers to pick up some ciggies."

I'd been around my uncle often enough to know he was lying through his teeth. But what did it matter? He was there. That's all I cared about.

The director irritated him even more by mentioning the choppy conditions and that rougher weather was on its way.

"It's fine. I know these waters like the back of my hand," said my uncle gritting his teeth.

When the director tried to engage my uncle about the movie outline he'd shown my mother earlier, he completely ignored him and began speaking fluent German to my mother in just the same way she did whenever she didn't want other people knowing what she was talking about. Thankfully, I understood German, so I could listen in to every word. My uncle didn't like the movie director and told her their story was no one's business but theirs.

Once they'd stopped talking in German, I asked my uncle how he'd learned to speak German like my mother. He explained they were both actually German by birth. I was surprised because when my mother earlier told me we were Jewish, I hadn't realized we were also German. As my uncle was telling me this, I noticed my mother locking eyes on him. It reminded me of her relief after he'd been rescued by the fishermen when I almost drowned as a four-year-old.

Out in the bay, the sea had become much rougher, and I could just make out a boat twisting and turning through the waves towards the secret beach. As it got closer to the jetty, I noticed its green and white hull and realized it was a Guardia Civil patrol boat. Next to me, my uncle was also closely studying the same vessel as it moored next to the jetty. He continued watching transfixed as the old Guardia Civil chief stood on the deck ready to disembark while two young officers tied the vessel up.

Back in the bar with one eye still on the jetty area, my uncle raised his bottle of beer to everyone else on the long table.

"Time for a toast," he bellowed. "To the death of that fucker Franco. Let's hope it's sooner rather than later because evil bastards like him will no longer rule the waves round here soon."

Moments after the crowd had given my uncle a hearty round of applause, the old chief walked in and headed to the main bar. He looked over and smiled at everyone before removing his black patent triangular hat and placing it carefully on the bar. Behind the counter, the New Zealander poured him a large cognac while looking across at my uncle.

The chief then turned towards everyone at the long table, raised his glass and said "Cheers" in a perfect English accent, which surprised me because I hadn't realized he spoke English. After that, I looked directly at my uncle, who nodded at Smelly. The New Zealander glanced across awkwardly at my uncle again and then poured more cognac into the chief's glass.

Everything seemed very tense all of a sudden. To try and lighten the atmosphere, I started strumming on my guitar again. Before I could get through a song, heavy rain drops began noisily smacking on the bar's tin roof. The thunder rumbling in the distance seemed to be moving towards us.

The chief remained on his own at the bar nursing his cognac and watching everyone as the New Zealander opened the till and counted some notes out, which he then put in an envelope and placed on the bar. The New Zealander caught my eye just after he'd done this, and I realized he must have been paying the old chief money. Later I discovered this was to avoid trouble with the Guardia Civil and other pro-Franco groups on the island.

The chief got up moments later, placed his black triangular hat carefully back on his head, picked up the envelope from the bar and nodded at the New Zealander. Then he walked off back towards the beach. At the long table, my uncle stood up and applauded loudly as I finished a song on my guitar. Then he proposed another toast, this time to the New Zealander, while he looked across at Smelly.

Down on the jetty, the chief boarded the Guardia Civil vessel while there was yet another exchange of furtive looks between my uncle, Smelly and the New Zealander in the beach bar. On the bridge of the Guardia Civil patrol boat, the chief took the radio transmitter receiver from one of his officers on the deck and spoke on it before shouting orders at the officer next to him on the bridge. He seemed angry and the vessel noisily fired up its engines.

Back on the long table, my uncle and his crew were shovelling mouthfuls of paella and swigging back more beers while still occasionally glancing down at the jetty. Below us, the Guardia Civil crew hurriedly cast off the vessel's ropes before it began edging out into the bay in reverse. Then it turned and headed forward with a surge through the rippling waves towards the increasingly rough waters further out beyond the shelter of the bay.

As my uncle and the New Zealander watched it, my mother leaned over and whispered something in my uncle's ear. I couldn't hear what it was, although he looked pissed off after she said it. Then she whispered something more to him in German, and this time I managed to catch it. I heard her say: "It had to be done. I had no choice."

My uncle seemed even more upset, turned away from her and sprang to his feet.

"Right lads," he said. "We've got an appointment in Tangiers. Let's get going."

The Hollywood director, still sitting directly opposite my mother, mentioned the bad weather again and even questioned the stability of the flat-bottomed MTB, saying they were notoriously unstable in rough weather.

My uncle smiled at me as if to say: "I wish this yank would shut the fuck up."

Then I asked him if I could go with him.

Before he had a chance to reply, my father interrupted and said it was "not a good idea".

"It's none of your fucking business," I said to my father.

My father rolled his eyes and then looked straight at my mother.

"You need to talk some sense into him," he told her.

I ignored them all and got up to leave with my uncle, but he immediately stopped me. Shrugging his shoulders, ruffling my hair like he always did and shaking his head, he said: "Let's do it another time, son."

I could tell from the serious tone of his voice that he meant it. Then he nodded at his two crew members, and they left the bar without another word.

I returned to the table. As I sat down, my mother yelled drunkenly at my father that he had no right to stop me doing anything. The director tried to intervene, and my father told him to fuck off and mind his own business. The director shrank into a ball and said nothing.

Down on the beach, my uncle and his two-man crew were approaching the jetty. Yet again, the so-called adults in my life were dealing with their own issues to the exclusion of me, so I didn't feel any of them had the right to decide what was best for me. So I darted out the back of the bar, through the kitchen and headed down towards the beach.

Ahead of me, I could see my uncle's friend Shorty untying the ropes on the jetty as Smelly pulled the gang plank on board. I knew where I wanted to be. On the bridge, my uncle was revving up the MTB's clunky old diesel engines. My father and his girlfriend had gone after me and were running along the beach about 50 yards behind me. I reached the jetty just as Smelly launched himself on to the MTB's deck and landed with a thump.

The engines grinded noisily as the boat held its position next to the jetty. I looked up at my uncle on the bridge. He seemed to be deliberately ignoring me, so I leapt onto the MTB's deck as it creaked loudly while rocking from side to side in the choppy water. On the bridge, my uncle looked down at me with a knowing grin on his face. He pushed the throttle forward to get the boat to reverse faster. Then he expertly swivelled the wheel so that we were facing out to sea and gradually pulled back the throttle.

My father and his girlfriend reached the jetty just as the MTB was pulling away. I didn't bother looking behind at my father as we surged, nose upwards out of the shelter of the enclosed bay towards the vast waves dominating the sea beyond. On the bridge, my uncle shook his head in mock disapproval as I approached. Then he laughed out loud as we smashed into the first of the larger waves rolling at us. It sent spray everywhere and the lumbersome old boat twisted to one side before levelling out.

My uncle shouted at Shorty to open a bottle of rum for the journey. It was only then I noticed that all the furniture inside the MTB had been stripped out and that it looked more like it must have when it was used during the war. In the lower cabin down the short steps, three balaclavas were discarded on the floor alongside two armoury boxes just like the ones I'd seen in the abandoned village with a skull and crossbones stencilled on them. One of them was open and contained three Tommy guns and two pistols, plus a handful of grenades and ammunition. It felt like we were about to embark on a lot more than a voyage down to Tangiers to pick up some duty-free cigarettes.

My uncle noticed me looking down into the cabin and shouted at me to come up and have some rum. As I climbed the steps to the bridge, Smelly turned to my uncle, tilted the bottle towards him and said: "All's clear on the Western Front, cap'n."

"Excellent, Smelter," said my uncle, taking a big swig of rum from the bottle. "Excellent."

It was only then I realized his name was Smelter and not Smelly. I was about to tell my uncle this when he passed the bottle to me with a big smile just as a massive wave crashed into the side of the MTB and sent us rolling from side to side. The hit of elation I felt from that rum, combined with the adrenaline as we surged through wave after wave towards the open sea, was more powerful than any of the drugs I'd taken during my short life.

CHAPTER SEVEN
STORMY WATERS

After the MTB reached the high seas beyond the craggy rocks that bordered both sides of the bay in front of the secret beach, there was no protection from the enormous waves raging around us. The sun peeping through a small gap in the clouds was dipping low behind the nearby hills and an almost full moon was gradually rising up over the opposite horizon, bathing the nearby rice swamps with a luminous grey light.

Once we'd passed the rocky peninsular on the edge of the bay, the flat-bottomed MTB began rolling from side to side even more as huge waves hit the hull and tossed us up into the air before we crashed back down into the angry sea. At the helm, my uncle was focused on the view ahead, though with the bottle of rum back in his hand. I grasped the rail on the bridge. He managed to smile at me reassuringly and handed me the bottle of rum.

A fierce gale whistled all around us and the rain felt like splinters of glass piercing my face. I could just make out rows of olive trees dotted up on the nearby stretch of fast-disappearing hillside. The trees were bending almost double in the storm. When the next wave hit us, the bottle of rum fell out of my grasp and onto the deck. It smashed into tiny pieces.

Moments later, an even bigger wave crashed over the boat. I lost my footing and was swept onto the deck and began sliding towards the open sea past Shorty. He stuck out a hand and somehow managed to grab me by the scruff of my neck and drag me back onto the bridge. As I struggled to get to my feet, I looked across at my uncle. This time he wasn't smiling. He seemed to be squinting at something ahead in the distance, so I turned to look in the same direction but couldn't see anything. The boat climbed high up into the air as another huge wave rolled under us.

When the MTB momentarily levelled out, I made out the distant lights of another similar-sized vessel partially illuminated in the moonlight, struggling through the storm towards us. Shorty and Smelter's eyes narrowed as they both looked in the direction of the other boat. My uncle then nodded at them, and they grabbed the rails while heading down to the lower deck.

On the bridge, my uncle began rotating the helm with his huge hands and the MTB started making a sharp 180-degree turn. We caught a wave sideways and masses of sea water swept across the entire deck before draining away.

On the lower deck, I watched avidly as Smelter and Shorty checked the ammunition in three Tommy guns and then cocked them. I was so transfixed by this that I didn't notice my uncle picking up a threadbare life jacket from a small storage cupboard beneath the helm. Before I'd even looked across at him, the life jacket landed at my feet as yet another wave rocked the boat from one side to the other.

"For fuck's sake put it on," screamed my uncle, as he wrestled the helm from side to side with his hands to try and encourage the MTB to ride the storm while watching the other vessel, which was still some distance behind us. We were in trouble, and for the first time that evening I wondered if the MTB could survive the storm, before a wall of water hit the side of the boat so hard that my uncle had to start frantically spinning the helm in the opposite direction to avoid us being capsized.

As I struggled to put the life jacket on, Smelter threw a Tommy gun to my uncle, who caught it one-handed despite the storm. He strapped it over his shoulder before looking behind to see where that other vessel was while another wave tossed the MTB up into the air like a toy. As we crashed back down into the sea, the unmistakable sound of the wooden hull splitting terrified me. The engines also seemed to be losing their power. The MTB was now listing so much to one side that I could see beneath the surface of the waves.

"Fucking jump," my uncle screamed at me.

I looked at him, unsure if he'd really just said that. I was frozen to the spot with fear.

"Do it, boy," he shouted.

As the boat leaned precariously to one side, I lost my balance and collided with my uncle, who was struggling to stand up next to me. With the boat still listing to one side, my uncle pushed me away so hard that I fell onto the deck just as another huge wave swept over the MTB. This sent me sliding towards the edge of the boat. Unable to scramble back, this time, I fell into the cold sea.

I remember glancing up as I crashed into the water and seeing Shorty and Smelter aiming their weapons in the direction of the other vessel behind us. I lost sight of them when another wave came in, picked me up and rolled me further away from the vessel's bright yellow hull, which was listing across the flickering moonlight before being tossed up into the air yet again.

The engines seemed to have stopped, and I gasped as the MTB almost completely rolled over, exposing a long split the entire length of the hull. As another huge wave took me some distance from the MTB, I could just make it out dipping beneath the surface. I desperately craned my neck to try and see if my uncle and his crew were in the water, but by that time I'd drifted too far away to see anything. It wasn't until another wave dragged me under the surface and then up again that I remembered my uncle couldn't swim.

As the latest wave pulled me beneath the surface again, I heard a buzzing noise. It seemed louder below the water line and sounded very much like the twin diesels of the vessel that we'd been trying to flee from. I just made out the outline of the same boat's bow ahead in the blackened distance riding on the crest of yet another enormous wave before it dipped nose first into the sea.

As it re-emerged, I could just make out its white and green markings in the partial moonlight, which confirmed to me that it had to be the same Guardia Civil boat from earlier. I should have been relieved someone was out there trying to rescue us, but instead I felt nothing but trepidation as I remembered how my uncle and his crew had armed themselves before trying to take the MTB in the opposite direction from the Guardia Civil vessel.

As I frantically looked around again for any sign of my uncle and his crew, the Guardia Civil boat appeared ahead of me. Though it was still quite a distance away, I could see its bow slicing through the waves as it headed in my direction. I looked around for my uncle's MTB yet again. It was still nowhere to be seen, but the police boat was approaching through the stormy seas just 50 yards in front of me.

Moments later, a length of bright orange rope looped through the air above me and landed in the water nearby. I tried and failed to grab hold of it twice. Then I finally managed to clasp it in my hand and was pulled towards the Guardia Civil vessel. Two men in yellow oilskins were leaning over the side of the boat urging me to hang on. As I reached up to them, the same two men hauled me onto the deck.

Once on the deck, I held onto railings with both my hands while one of my rescuers signalled to an officer on the bridge through the driving rain. The vessel made a sharp turn and headed in the opposite direction away from where I'd seen my uncle's MTB go down.

I looked up at both my rescuers and begged them in Spanish to turn back. They ignored me. Then they grabbed my arms and pulled me to my feet and pushed me towards a door with a port hole. On the other side of that door was a small cabin. Once inside it, they placed me roughly in a chair and handcuffed me to one of the arms. One of them said in Spanish it was for my own safety because of the storm, but it didn't feel that way. As they stood over me, the door to the cabin swung open and the old Guardia Civil chief from the beach bar earlier walked in. But this time he wasn't smiling.

I asked him about my uncle and the rest of the crew. He shook his head and just said "all gone" in English. Then he looked down at me and asked me in Spanish what the MTB had been carrying. I said I didn't know. Then he leaned in so close to me I could smell the New Zealander's cheap beach bar cognac still on his breath, and he said: "Drogas, hombre. Drogas", before leaving. One of the two younger officers who'd dragged me to the cabin stood behind me and pulled so hard on my ponytail that my head jerked backwards. Then he spat in my face before leaving and locking the door behind him.

My head seemed to be constantly spinning as the Guardia Civil boat rocked from side to side through the stormy seas for at least half an hour. I remember blacking out for a few minutes and then coming round again as the boat's engines began fading in strength, which meant we were approaching Ibiza's Old Town port.

After the Guardia Civil boat moored, I was dragged up to the deck by the same two young officers and onto the shore. The older Guardia Civil man nodded towards a waiting green and white Seat van. That took me to the Guardia Civil headquarters, where I was thrown into a cell in my soaking clothes, still trying to work out why they were treating me this way. I knew it was bad, but I was more concerned with where my uncle and his crew were.

My mother and uncle and our life on Ibiza had taught me never to trust the Guardia Civil. But I was in a state of suspended disbelief by this time. Was this all to do with settling old civil war scores? Were those accusations of drug smuggling just an excuse to get at my family?

At 6 a.m. the following morning, the same two younger officers entered my cell and began asking me over and over again about the drugs they said were in the MTB. They kept telling me I'd be sent to prison for years for drug smuggling. I denied all knowledge of drugs, which was easy because I knew nothing about them and doubted they even existed. The officer who'd spat in my face on the boat did it again and told me I'd be locked up until I confessed everything to them. Then they slammed the cell door behind them.

Later that same day, two more officers entered my cell, handcuffed me and took me through the back of the building to where another green and white van was waiting. I was pushed into the back and told to keep quiet. Were they taking me somewhere to kill me? I knew the Guardia Civil were capable of anything.

For 15 minutes the van slowly made its way through the old town's narrow lanes, as I tried to imagine what my fate would be. As we left the town, I concluded they were probably taking me somewhere deserted out in the campo. By this time, the van was moving along a narrow track near the rice fields, and I could see through the window that the sea had completely calmed. It was as if the huge storm from just a few hours earlier had never happened.

We eventually stopped close to a crowd of at least a dozen Guardia Civil officers gathered near the edge of the sea next to assorted patrol cars, a mechanical digger and a tractor. Had those machines already dug my grave? Was this where it would all end?

It wasn't until I got out of the van that I saw the upturned yellow hull of my uncle's MTB boat beached on the sand beyond the Guardia Civil officers. The sight of it sent a different kind of shock wave through me because it reminded me of what I'd just been through, as well as of my uncle and the other crew members. I hoped that maybe they'd been rescued after all.

The chief was among the group of officers. He turned to watch me approaching with my guards. After we reached him, he smiled and ordered the two young officers to remove my handcuffs. Once again speaking in perfect English, he apologized for what I'd been through and calmly explained that it was very important that they recovered everything that had been on the boat when it sank. He said they'd found some guns and grenades, but he wanted to know where my uncle had hidden the drugs. I again insisted I knew nothing about them.

As the driver of the rusting old digger fired up his engine and slowly lifted one end of the split hull in order to turn it upright, masses of sea water began surging out of it. Moments later, the chief nodded at the same two younger officers, who grabbed me by each arm and moved me next to the battered wooden deck. The chief looked straight at me while nodding and smiling at the same time.

"We will find it all in the end," he said, without a hint of emotion in his voice.

When I didn't respond, the chief signalled to the two officers and they took me to the van. During the first five minutes of the drive, I asked the driver in Spanish three times where we were going, but he said nothing. I was imagining that this time they really were taking me somewhere to kill me because I'd refused to co-operate.

So when the van ended up on the main road back towards the Old Town, I was relieved because that meant we were heading back to the Guardia Civil headquarters. On arrival, two guards escorted me back down towards the cells in the basement. I begged them to let me use a toilet. But they refused and pushed me roughly into the cells before locking me in. I couldn't hold out any longer and ended up sprawled out on the ice-cold stone floor in a puddle of my own urine. But despite this, I was so exhausted I eventually managed to drift to sleep.

* * *

I don't remember what I dreamt about that night, but I was woken up by a bucketful of water thrown in my face by a Guardia Civil officer. Being back in reality felt far worse than any nightmare. Standing behind the Guardia Civil officer was the chief sneering at me, while he watched through the bars of my cell. Then he marched in and calmly stood over me with his arms crossed.

"You're a lucky man," he said. "You're being released without charge."

I presumed the New Zealander had pulled a few strings to get me out.

When I stepped into the bright sunshine from the Guardia Civil headquarters later that morning, there were no familiar faces to greet me. Instead, a large shiny black Seat with tailfins and glistening chrome was parked up in front of the building, with two men in lightweight suits leaning against the front wing. They beckoned me over.

The back door to the car then swung open and an older British voice told me to get in. When I peered into the car, the man sitting there immediately looked familiar. It was the skinny, middle-class-looking man who wore wire-rimmed specs that made him look like a college professor whom I'd first met at that Soho book launch I'd attended with my uncle.

"We need to talk," he said, as I hesitated about getting in the Seat until the two men in lightweight suits appeared either side of me.

The car set off through the narrow, cobbled back streets of the Old Town. The British gangster told me what a "great bloke" my uncle was. How all the international brigades people on the island were special characters, who'd all stuck together, despite losing the war, and how impressive that had been.

"I was too young to have fought in it, thank gawd," he said. "They reckon it was a romantic war but I don't get that because a war is a fucking war and people die. What's romantic about that?"

His tone sounded a bit weary. As if he'd heard the old vets say it many times before.

"But now this island is a tourist destination, things are changing. I'm what you might call the new generation of foreign entrepreneurs on Ibiza. We pride ourselves on getting rich from the import export game."

Then he paused.

"Anyway, you're now responsible for the drugs that were on your uncle's boat," he said. "And they're worth a minimum of £100,000."

"My uncle hated drugs and would never have had anything to do with them," I gulped.

The gangster (as I now knew he was a gangster) laughed when I said that. I wondered why I'd not seen him before on the island, but I wasn't connected to the Ibiza underworld, so why would I have known him? Then he asked me if my uncle had stopped off anywhere after sailing off from the secret beach that evening. I told him the weather had been so bad that all we'd wanted to do was get to Morocco as quickly as possible.

"How about before he arrived at the beach that afternoon?" he asked. "Did he mention going anywhere on the way there?"

I said I had no idea.

What was happening to me was completely out of my comfort zone. I was a laidback, peace-loving, idealistic young drug-taking hippy-type from Ibiza, not a professional criminal. And I'd just fallen into a trap that would change my life forever.

ACT II

ACCIDENTAL DRUG LORD

1975–2002

CHAPTER EIGHT
THE DEBT

The Brit's car eventually pulled up outside my mother's villa. He must have known exactly where she lived, because he never asked for directions. I'd just opened the door of the Seat when he stopped me and announced that he needed to talk to my mother "in case she knows what happened to my drugs". I said she was very ill and asked him to wait while I went inside to talk to her first, as I knew how upset she'd be about my uncle's death.

He looked at me for a moment, as if I was the most naïve person he'd ever met.

"I'm not asking," he said.

"Please. I need to make sure she's okay."

He looked me up and down in an inquisitive way, no doubt trying to suss out whether I was trying to pull a fast one.

"Okay," he finally said.

Relieved, I let myself into the house. Most of the shutters were closed, so it was virtually pitch black despite the sunshine. I waited for a few moments for my mother to appear, but when she didn't, I headed on tiptoes up to her bedroom. As I suspected, she'd taken to her bed distraught about what had happened and appeared to be asleep, unaware of the Brit's car still waiting outside.

Then she opened her eyes, stared at me for a few moments and then asked if it was really me or was she dreaming. After I nodded, she sat up and hugged me tightly and started crying, which I'd never seen her do before in my entire life. She eventually told me that the Guardia Civil had informed her that I'd also drowned along with my uncle and his two mates. It must have felt to her as if I'd just come back from the dead.

Moments later, the Brit knocked on the front door. She asked who it was and I told her to stay in the bedroom while I dealt with it. She was in no fit state to disagree. I opened the front door gingerly because I wanted him to believe that my mother was in a bad way. Then I ushered him into the front yard. At first he grimaced at me for defying him, and it felt like he was about to do something to me, before he noticed my mother watching us from her bedroom window. She looked as white as a sheet and tears were still rolling down her cheeks.

He glanced at her for a few moments, then said he'd come back another time. Before he left, he turned round. Looking into my eyes, he told me that I had one month to return the missing drugs to him or find the money to pay for them. As I watched the Brit's car drive off on the dusty track it all hit me like an Exocet missile, and I wondered what the fuck was going on.

Back inside the villa, my mother was refusing to come out of her bedroom. I was so shattered I didn't press her and instead went into my own room, lay down on the bed and fell asleep almost instantly.

I woke up hours later to the sound of someone hammering on the front door. I stumbled out of bed to find the New Zealander on the doorstep wanting to see if we were okay. I persuaded him to have a cigarette with me outside before we went in and saw my mother.

I explained everything that had happened since I'd left his beach on my uncle's MTB. He listened carefully, but the expression on his face remained unchanged throughout, even when I recalled my encounter with the chief and the one-month deadline to find the drugs I hadn't even known existed. I even mentioned having met the Brit before with my uncle at that criminal's book launch in Soho. The New Zealander immediately shook his head and said that I must have got him mixed up with someone else. Then he clapped me on the back in a friendly manner.

"This isn't about drugs, son," said the New Zealander. "Nothing's going to happen to you. It's just a misunderstanding."

The way the New Zealander explained it convinced me, though, that there had been something on that boat, even if it wasn't drugs. Then he asked me to say hello to my mother from him and left before I'd had a chance to ask him anything else.

That evening I cooked my mother a meal. She hadn't eaten anything since that last fateful plate of paella on the secret beach three days earlier and seemed grateful. We drank a bottle of wine between us, and I tried to talk to her about what had happened. She insisted that she knew nothing about what was on board the MTB and that my uncle would never have got involved with drugs, but I could tell she was holding something back.

I went to bed at around midnight, and as I was closing the shutters to my bedroom window, I noticed a car parked in the distance, illuminated by the moonlight. I could just make out the orange glow of a cigarette coming from inside it and realized someone was sitting there watching the villa.

* * *

The following morning, I woke up very early and the car outside the villa had gone. I was so spaced out from everything that had happened that I wondered for a few moments if I'd imagined it all. Then the cold, harsh reality of my situation kicked in. I had to find out very quickly what was in my uncle's boat because it was threatening my very existence. It wasn't just about the Brit's deadline to find his alleged missing drugs, either. There was a myriad of questions, including why had my uncle really been in Ibiza that weekend? What was he carrying on his MTB? And why were the Guardia Civil and now a British drug lord so interested?

But where should I start? In the end I chose to begin at the most obvious place in the hope it might at least point me in the right direction. I slipped quietly out of the villa so as not to wake my mother and headed on foot towards the water-logged rice fields. Soon, I could see the upturned yellow hull of my uncle's beached MTB in the distance, backlit by the early morning sun flickering lazily across the rippling sea.

As I approached the wreck, I checked around to make sure all the police had gone. After reaching it, I walked around it a couple of times while I ran through everything that had happened. It seemed so surreal knowing that just three days earlier, I'd been on that same boat in a storm that ended up turning my life upside down.

I stopped by a ripped hole in the side of the boat and used it to get a foothold in order to clamber onto the crumbling deck. Once I was on it, I lit a cigarette and studied two of the wooden boxes that had so recently contained guns and grenades but were now empty. Why had they been armed that night? And why had the chief been ready and waiting for us in his patrol boat as we left the bay? The questions just kept coming.

Whatever happened, there was no way that my uncle had had time to throw any drugs overboard as the Guardia Civil boat closed in on the MTB in that storm. But none of this helped me focus on the task at hand as I stood there.

I was about to head back to my mother's villa when I heard a couple of cormorants squawking noisily in the bullrushes close to the beached wreck. Then I noticed at least a dozen gulls hovering above them. It looked as if they'd found something in the sand.

Unable to make out what it was, I moved closer as other birds swooped in and began jostling for the air space where the gulls were fluttering. As I approached, many of them flew off, leaving a couple of bigger gulls, who landed on something hidden by the bullrushes, which they seemed to be trying to peck at. I hesitated for a few moments as another flock of gulls turned up and started dive-bombing the same spot because they wanted a piece of whatever it was that lay on the sand beneath them. They eventually flew off, leaving something crumpled up on the waterlogged sand.

It was only when I got about 20 feet away that I made out the shredded remains of a porpoise. The birds had pecked its eyes out and dug deep holes over the entire blubbery corpse, exposing flesh and gristle. I felt my stomach retch, caught my breath and walked off, relieved that it hadn't been my uncle or one of his crew lying there.

* * *

I was so shaken by seeing the wreck again that I decided to head into Ibiza Old Town for a drink, although it wasn't even lunchtime. I needed something to calm my nerves. I'd been given a month to find a drug baron's supply or be killed, and I'd just lost one of the most important people in my life.

My route into the Old Town would normally take me past the old bullring. However, as I walked along the tree-lined main road, I was astonished to see that the bullring was no longer there. I noticed a couple of orange mechanical diggers at the main entrance area systematically demolishing the remains of the perimeter wall of the arena. Five or six Guardia Civil officers stood around barking instructions to digger drivers as to where they needed to keep smashing down the concrete.

As one huge wall collapsed, I could clearly see past it to where the auditorium used to be, but there was just rubble and clouds of dust from other machines working inside. I decided to take a closer look, but within about 25 yards, one of the Guardia Civil officers approached me with his hand up to stop me going any nearer the bullring. I instinctively turned to walk away from him, but he quickly caught up with me and warned me to leave the area immediately. When I asked him why they'd demolished the bullring, he hesitated before saying it was dangerous and no longer safe for people to enter.

While walking back towards the main road, I met an old man wearing a black beret, who'd also been watching the demolition from a distance. He told me that the demolition had begun a few weeks earlier but was then stopped for a few days after something was discovered beneath the main stand. He said he'd seen the Guardia Civil loading boxes and sacks onto trucks late at night. When I asked him what they'd found, he said it must have been the bodies of those executed at the bullring during the civil war. He said the Guardia Civil wanted to hide evidence of war crimes by the fascists because everyone knew that once Franco died, there would be international pressure for his fascist followers to be brought to justice.

I didn't know how to respond to what he told me, so I wished him good day and walked back on to the dusty side of the main, tree-lined road into the Old Town. I kept thinking about what the old man had said to me, though. It all connected to my mother's fear of the bullring and how she'd always tried to stop my father taking me there. But then I got irritated with myself because it felt like a huge diversion from the matter at hand, which concerned a load of missing drugs that needed to be found if I wanted to live a long and healthy life.

I was so immersed in all this as I walked slowly into the Old Town that I didn't even notice a couple of people I knew sitting at a roadside bar until they began shouting to me. If I'd spotted them earlier, I think I would most likely have ducked out of sight because I didn't really want to see anyone. But they insisted on me joining them for a beer, and once the alcohol kicked in, I started to feel a little more relaxed about everything. After a couple more beers, one of them slipped a sachet of powdered speed into my hand under the table. I didn't hesitate to take it because I needed an escape from everything for a few hours. That amphetamine wasn't exactly going to help clear my head, but at least I'd be able to obliterate what had just happened, albeit temporarily.

Within another hour, I'd drunk half a bottle of cheap brandy and bought some drugs for myself. I was in the mood for a good session. My binge turned into a tour of all the Old Town's seediest hole-in-the-wall bars. I was trying to kill the pain and push everything out of my mind, but actually all it did was make me think even more vividly about what had happened.

Twelve hours later, I was slumped in the toilet of a tatty nightclub on the edge of the Old Town barely conscious when I heard what I presumed were two policemen smashing on the doors of all the cubicles demanding that all the occupants come out. I kept quiet and tried to flush the drugs down the toilet but fell over and cracked my head on the side of the bowl. Two men kicked the door open, and I waited to have the crap beaten out of me. Instead, the Brit walked into the cubicle, picked my wallet up off the floor, handed it to me and ordered his two men to help me to a waiting car. As they dragged me out of the back exit of the club, I asked them where we were heading, but they ignored me. Perhaps the Brit had decided to make an example of me after all and not bother waiting for that one-month deadline to expire?

I must have lost consciousness after they bundled me into that waiting car, because I woke up about 24 hours later in a sparsely furnished bedroom. I stumbled to my feet and tried to open the shutters, but they were nailed up. Then I heard the door to the bedroom being unlocked and one of the two men who'd dragged me out of the nightclub walked in with a coffee and a fresh bread roll with apricot jam. He put it on the bedside table and left, locking the door behind him.

As I wolfed it down, I heard a car pull up outside. That sparked a rush of paranoia, which heightened when the Brit reappeared and calmly informed me that he was still waiting for his missing shipment of drugs and that getting wasted wasn't going to help either of us. He also said that he'd put some money in my mother's bank account to make sure she could pay her bills and that now I needed to get out of bed and help him find his supply.

There were no threats, but then he didn't need to raise his voice because the message was loud and clear. It wasn't as if I could go to the police to ask for help, either, because they were in his pocket. The Brit said he wouldn't approach my mother as long as I started making a proper effort to find his "missing narcotics" (as he liked to call them). He warned me that if I tried to disappear then he wouldn't hesitate to pay her a visit.

They dropped me at my mother's villa that afternoon. I found her sitting staring into space in the kitchen. She didn't even acknowledge me at first, but I noticed that the back window overlooking the garden had been smashed. I asked what had happened, but she still didn't respond. After a long silence, she asked me to pour her some wine. Her hands were shaking as she held the glass in her hand.

After two big gulps, she took a deep breath and told me the Guardia Civil chief had turned up at the villa. She'd pretended she wasn't in, and his men had broken the window to get in the house. The chief told her that my uncle hadn't died and that he'd stolen a shipment of missing drugs before he'd sailed off from the secret beach that day. The chief and his men had then searched the house but found nothing.

"Do you think he's still alive?" my mother asked after telling me all this.

I shrugged my shoulders and said it was possible but not very likely after what we'd gone through during that storm.

"I bet he does reappear," she said, almost proudly. "He's done it before. He'll do it again."

As she started on her fourth glass of wine in less than 30 minutes, I noticed her hand no longer shook. It hadn't been caused by the police raid but by her addiction to alcohol.

After my mother had gone back to bed – as she often did when she was upset – I phoned the Brit and asked him to talk to the chief and tell him to leave her alone.

"That old bastard's up to something. I'll handle him," he said, before reminding me that the clock was still ticking for the return of his "narcotics".

It's a strange feeling to know that someone plans to kill you if you don't find something that you didn't know existed in the first place. I felt kind of helpless. I knew I had to get a grip of myself and start actively looking for answers. The Brit's deadline was a fact of life and there was absolutely nothing I could do about it. I couldn't just wait there for him to come and get me.

I managed a solid 12 hours sleep that night and woke up fresh and determined to start piecing everything together, even though I wasn't confident of discovering the truth, especially as it seemed to centre around my uncle. I discovered from one pothead friend on the island that the Brit had actually been Ibiza's main cannabis supplier for at least three years but few people knew him because he had teams of dealers out doing his dirty work for him. My friend put me in touch with one of those dealers. He turned out to be a middle-aged German hippy, and we met in a bar in the Old Town. This guy warned me the Brit was not someone to cross. When I asked him what this meant, he ran the tip of his finger across his own neck and laughed. I had no idea if he was trying to wind me up or not.

After that, I headed to American Joe's commune where I'd once been to school in the hope he might know what had been on the MTB.

"Your uncle was a law unto himself," he explained. "Who knows what he might have been smuggling on that boat. And remember he had a lot of enemies here and in London."

"What sort of enemies?" I asked American Joe.

"The type you don't want to go round asking questions about," he said.

After spending a week talking to people, I was no nearer to finding out what was on the MTB, and then I spotted the Brit in the centre of Ibiza Old Town with two henchmen in tow. I ducked down an alleyway to avoid him and then cut back across two narrow lanes just to be sure he didn't find me. I'd just turned into a small plaza on the edge of the Old Town when I walked straight into his two henchmen. They escorted me back to a small hole-in-the-wall bar where the Brit was waiting. He got straight to the point and warned me to be careful about asking questions around town because people might think I was a police officer and that could be bad for his business.

"But I suppose at least you're trying, son," he said, flicking some dust off my shoulders.

Then he made a point of saying to me: "Someone knows where my narcotics are and I want them back", before asking me to run a few errands for him that were not connected to the missing drugs. I had to keep on the right side of him, so I agreed.

Those "errands" included picking up cash from the gang's street dealers who worked in and around Ibiza Old Town and San Antonio, the other big town on the island. I was even lent a car. After delivering all the takings from the cannabis sales to him at the end of the following day, he reminded me I was "still on probation", but at least he didn't mention the missing drugs again. But then, in many ways, he already had me in the palm of his hand.

After three or four days of running errands for him it dawned on me that the Brit's supplies of cannabis did not seem to have been depleted by the missing shipment that was hanging over me. Surely he would have run out of drugs by now if that cannabis on board the MTB was missing?

Questions. Questions. But no answers.

Over the following couple of weeks, I got stopped several times by the Guardia Civil on the pretext of checking my documents. When it happened for the fourth time in five days, I realized this was the old chief's way of reminding me that I was still in his sights and that there was absolutely nothing I could do about it.

I'd hit a dead-end and almost completely run out of ideas.

Three days before the deadline was due to expire, I was roped in by the Brit to help pick up a load of cannabis from a deserted beach on the sparsely populated north-west side of the island. He wasn't there and the pick-up was led by a fat

French guy who worked for the Brit. He seemed to know all about my predicament, so as we drove back across the island to the Old Town, I asked him what the fuck I should do. I had nothing to lose by this stage, and what was the harm in making sure the Brit heard that I really didn't know where his missing drugs were?

The Frenchman said he felt sorry for me but I needed to be very careful about upsetting the Brit. He advised me never to mention the missing drugs again and to hope that the Brit didn't go through with his threat. After the Frenchman told me all this, I felt even more depressed about my predicament, and I had absolutely no one to turn to. I realized then I was ill-equipped to deal with these criminals and was caught up in a vicious drugs underworld that was completely alien to me.

* * *

The day before my one-month deadline was set to expire, I spent a sleepless night going round and round in my head everything that had happened in the days and weeks before the sinking. But it didn't help make anything clearer.

Deadline day came and went without any comment from the Brit, though. I was surprised but didn't dare tempt fate by mentioning it. So I continued running more errands for him, assuming that everything was now maybe ironed out. We seemed to be getting on well, although I still had no doubt that if I tried to leave the gang, he'd come after me and my mother, so I never once thought about running. Whatever was happening, it was much better than fearing for my life, so I let it continue.

After another couple of weeks of driving across the island picking up cash from cannabis dealers and dropping off small amounts of pot to many of the same dealers, the Brit invited me to visit a warehouse that he used as a storage depot. I was convinced this was the moment he was finally going to announce he was taking action against me over his missing drugs.

It must have been obvious I was worried, because as soon as I walked into his office, he slapped me on the back in a friendly manner and announced that I was now a full-time member of his gang. The Brit casually informed me there was no salary to go with my new job, as I was paying off my drug debt to him, although he said he'd continue to put money into my mother's account so she would be okay. He also told me he'd give me small amounts of cash for my expenses, although it would never be enough to give me much freedom. And then he said: "All I want in return is a promise that if you come across my narcotics then you will return them to their rightful owner.

I nodded and went with the flow. Despite having been thrust into the underworld through no choice of my own, I felt that a lot of what had happened was down to me. I'd pushed my uncle to let me go with him on his MTB that afternoon. He hadn't really wanted me on board, probably because of something he had on that boat. I'd refused to take no for an answer, and now I needed to face up to the consequences of those actions.

It didn't sit easily with me to be a criminal, but I had to accept that the Brit was now my boss and I was going to have to do pretty much anything he wanted in order to remain alive. I was soon promoted to transporting drugs as well as packing them onto a vehicle, and also driving my new boss all over the island. He said I was the best driver in the gang, and since he was an extremely nervous passenger, I took that as a compliment.

The only thing I said I would never do was resort to any violence on his behalf. The Brit assured me that the cannabis business rarely involved it, unlike cocaine, which he insisted he'd always studiously avoided for that very same reason.

"In any case," said the Brit. "You wouldn't be any good at threatening someone because you need to sound as if you really mean it."

The way he said that reminded me he was more than capable of doing it himself if he had to.

Everyone in the gang had their own specific roles, and the Brit deliberately made sure that we knew very little about anything beyond our own actual duties within that infrastructure. This was primarily done to ensure that no individual gang member could inform on the rest of the gang and its operations if they were ever arrested by the police or kidnapped by rivals, who might end up resorting to torturing us for such information.

I got the slight impression that my British boss had someone else above him, who might not have been based in Ibiza. I had no idea who that was, and it was better not to know because that would have put me right in the firing line, if there was ever a fallout.

* * *

I managed to stay off recreational drugs myself throughout those early days in the gang. This endeared me not only to the Brit but also to my mother, who'd spent years trying to stop me taking drugs. My new boss was right about us not taking drugs, though. Being straight helped when it came to retaining focus and ensuring we made few errors during the course of our work. In this game, one mistake could prove extremely costly. The Brit summed it up when a few weeks after my "full-time appointment" he announced to me that I should always remember we were in the business of drugs "but the drugs should never own us". And throughout this period, he continued talking up how dealing in cannabis wasn't really against the law, as far as he was concerned.

Obviously, my mother knew what I was doing because of the money being paid into her bank account, as well as the strange hours I was "working" and the fancy car I often arrived home in. However, she never asked me directly where it was all coming from, so the peace was kept. And meanwhile, I still kept wondering if she knew a lot more about what was on my uncle's MTB than she was admitting.

In the space of a few months, I'd gone from being an out-of-work young, idealistic Ibiza flower-power teenager into a full-time employee of the island's most successful drug baron. Yet I had little money to show for it because I was paying off a huge debt on a load of missing drugs I knew nothing about. I kept pinching myself to try and get my head round everything that had happened. It was a complete mindfuck.

CHAPTER NINE
FILLING THE VACUUM

About six months after my uncle's drowning – in November 1975 – General Franco finally died. Ibiza and the rest of Spain should have been celebrating, but his death did little to help heal the nation's deep divisions when it came to the conflicts hanging over from the civil war. Ibiza was expected to open up following the death of Franco. Instead, his passing left a huge vacuum, with people on both sides of the political divide trying to cash in on the nation's hesitancy about returning to free and fair elections.

Mainland Spain went into a state of limbo in the months following Franco's death. Many believed that his iron fist had kept a lot of old enemies apart from each other and that that had helped prevent any complicated internal conflicts from flaring up. They were convinced that now Franco was dead, the hatred from both sides would come out into the open even more and lead to a new civil war, as political opponents sought to settle scores with their old enemies.

Meanwhile, Franco's beloved Guardia Civil remained at the helm of Ibiza's law enforcement effort, despite fears that some citizens would rise up against them and the old pro-Franco politicians who encouraged them to stay. Characters like the chief – who was in the pocket of my boss – remained in charge of the island's main police force, despite all the rumours which had swirled around him for decades, including his supposed role in the disappearances of dozens of enemies of General Franco before, during and after the civil war.

Many on the island had presumed the chief would flee Ibiza. Instead, he made it clear he was determined to stay on and run the Guardia Civil. He saw it as his territory, and no one was going to take it away from him. His officers often helped unload cannabis shipments as well as providing armed security when we met with our Moroccan pot suppliers during their visits to Ibiza.

There were a number of prominent local left-wing politicians on the island unwilling to kick the chief out. My boss told me with a smile one day that the old goat had kept files on many of his enemies down the years and they feared he might expose them. My boss made it crystal clear to me that keeping that old chief in power was very much to our advantage and an integral part of his cannabis operation. Because without him, he said, we'd have big problems with law enforcement. I tried not to think about how I'd ended up working for a criminal gang in league with the same man who'd refused to help try and rescue my own uncle as his boat sank.

The vacuum left by Franco's death actually helped increase the tidal wave of drugs flooding into Ibiza and the rest of Spain. It was a lot easier to smuggle narcotics when much of the nation's law enforcement infrastructure on the mainland was in disarray.

My boss was running an efficient and highly profitable cannabis business, which I was now an integral part of. And we got on well, although I was still paying off that huge debt to him as part of my deal. There were moments when my boss showed a remarkably generous side to his character, though. When I found out that my mother's villa was actually legally owned by my uncle after the bank threatened to repossess it unless I came up with £5,000 to pay off the mortgage on it, my boss immediately stepped in and provided the money for her. He did point out it would have to go against my future earnings for the gang, but I was thankful for his faith, nonetheless.

Becoming a criminal continued to have very little to do with my own personal greed. It was simply a means to an end, a way to settle the debts that me and my dysfunctional family had incurred, plus of course the shipment of drugs I knew nothing about and would be paying off for some years to come.

The gang itself had the exclusive rights to cannabis distribution on Ibiza throughout this period of time. This monopoly meant that the Brit was able to set up lucrative deals with Moroccan cannabis suppliers without treading on the toes of other gangsters, as there simply weren't any other significant drug lords on the island at that time. My boss also developed big plans to turn Ibiza into a transportation hub for importing cannabis, which could then be shipped onto other more lucrative markets in Europe and beyond. The potential profits for this were vast. One ton of cannabis bought in Morocco for £10,000 had a street value of at least £100,000 in Europe at that time. And that was before it was repackaged and redistributed for the commercial market, which could further double its value.

I must confess I found the mechanics of drug dealing on such a vast scale fascinating. It wasn't just a matter of the cannabis turning up on a boat from Morocco and then being pushed on elsewhere. We had to carefully repackage the product and make sure it was sealed airtight. This was to prevent the drugs being sniffed out by police dogs, since much of our product was shipped on to Europe by lorry from the mainland and those vehicles had to pass through the closely controlled customs posts of at least three countries.

About a year after I first started working for the Brit, he opened a furniture and kitchen equipment business on the island as a cover. The company was based in a brand-new vast warehouse, packed to the rafters with cheap household and office furniture, as well as kitchen equipment. He had a mezzanine office with a glass window overlooking the rest of the inside of the building.

There was a definite art to disguising cannabis because it was so bulky. You couldn't just sling it in a few holdalls and hope for the best. The Brit devised a genius method which involved packing hash in bricks wrapped in cling film which were then constructed into the shape of a sofa or an armchair and disguised with an outer layer of foam cushions. This had a tightly fitting cover stretched over it and nailed to the main frame. Those covers had to be soaked in perfume to be doubly certain any inspections with dogs would not detect them.

The gang specifically trained one of those same *podenco ibicenco* dogs like the one I had as a child to sniff out cannabis in our shipments before they were dispatched. If the hound managed to find any, the Brit would order us to repack the entire load and the dog was used to test it all over again. The cannabis sofas and chairs were transported among other real pieces of furniture on lorries that even had the Brit's furniture and kitchen equipment livery on their sides.

My apprenticeship in the drug business ended up lasting two years because that was how long it took me to pay off all my debts to the Brit. In fairness, he let me off the last 25 per cent of money owed and my uncle's missing drugs were no longer ever mentioned. I felt at the time that I'd been extremely lucky to have turned a threat against my life into a full-time job.

And when I finally received my first full pay packet from the gang, I'd become so institutionalized that the drugs underworld seemed perfectly normal to me, despite all my earlier misgivings. My boss began paying me £3,000 cash every month and a bonus on top sometimes. Yet despite now being properly paid, money itself still meant precious little to me. I wasn't interested in possessions like cars and clothes. I didn't spend anything on drugs for myself because I'd long since kicked all that into touch in accordance with the gang not taking narcotics. My first few pay packets ended up going on doing up my mother's villa.

About two and a half years after my uncle's MTB sank, my father turned up back in Ibiza from London for the first time since that day on the beach. He was still with the same German girlfriend he'd had since splitting from my mother. We'd became virtually estranged after I'd defied him to go with my uncle that day, so it was no big surprise when he started lecturing me about being in a drugs gang. He predicted that I'd end up in prison or dead.

At first, I was actually oddly touched that he seemed to genuinely care about me, even though I didn't particularly want to hear what he was saying. But then he took the conversation onto a different level by blaming my uncle for it all. He said he was sick of hearing what a great man my uncle had been and believed that it was his "dodgy business deals" that had led to the sinking of the MTB and my subsequent emergence as a criminal.

And of course he was right in many ways. But attacking my uncle seemed insensitive to me because, after all, he was no longer with us. So I confronted him about what he meant by that. He paused for a moment and seemed to be on the verge of opening up when he thought better of it and told me to talk to my mother "about all that".

"So why are you really here?" I asked him.

He looked sheepishly at me and admitted he'd had to leave the UK "in a hurry" after being banned from every casino in London after losing vast sums of money gambling. Debt collectors had been turning up on his doorstep and he seemed genuinely afraid to return to the UK.

I was shocked to hear all this from my father. Despite everything, I didn't like seeing him in such a vulnerable state, so I let him and his girlfriend stay in a villa I was renting with my excess cash and moved back in full time with my mother, whose health at this time had been steadily deteriorating thanks to her consumption of alcohol and tranquilizers. I had plenty of spare money, so I agreed to help my father repay his debts, just as long as he stopped lecturing me about my life of crime.

I suppose the real reason I helped him was because I'd felt so sorry for him during so much of my childhood. He was often pushed into the background by my mother and her International Brigades friends. The only way he could get her full attention was to defy her like he did when he made up that Hollywood actor's autobiography. I think doing that book had been a cry for attention from my father, but my mother saw it as a petulant act of defiance.

I seemed to be increasingly supporting my parents. The trouble was that this meant being in a drugs gang had become essential to my family's survival. While I'd never imagined leaving the gang, I was now trapped in a vicious circle. My career in the drugs business had actually become an essential distraction from my problems at home and the conflicting feelings I had about my parents. I was increasingly wedded to it financially and emotionally.

Most of my supposedly real friends on the island had long since been referring to me as a "bad person" behind my back because they knew I was in the drugs business. Yet I considered dealing in cannabis to be no different from selling alcohol, so it had seemed a harsh reaction to me at first, but there was little I could do about it. As a result, my boss, the Brit, and his drug gang became much more of a home to me socially as well. I felt safer and less judged when I was with them. We understood each other. We knew how far to press each other's buttons and it felt like a genuine element of friendship existed between us.

Back at home, I'd tried my hardest not to involve my mother in any aspect of my life of crime since I'd first joined the gang three years earlier. She came from a generation that lumped all narcotics together as being something suspicious and evil. One time, I tried to explain to her that cannabis was probably less addictive than alcohol, but it went right over her head.

There was one other person in my life who knew exactly what I did for a living and had never tried to judge me, so I invited my best and only friend from school to stay with me in Ibiza for a couple of weeks. During some crazy nights out together, we discussed just about everything, from my involvement in the drugs game to his difficult relationship with his father, who was still the president of the DRWA. He even cheered my mother up by accompanying us to the New Zealander's secret beach most days.

The last night before he returned to London, he pleaded with me to walk away from the drugs trade. I was quite surprised because he'd never voiced any disapproval of it before, although I knew he'd been training as a lawyer back in the UK.

"It's going to go badly wrong," he said.

I hesitated to respond and then side-stepped the question, which reminded me of just how institutionalized I'd become by the drugs game. He warned me that I'd end up in prison if I wasn't careful. But was that such a bad thing? Then he urged me to return to London with him and get what he described as a proper job. But I was being paid a lot of money and both my parents needed supporting. When I told him that, he laughed and described that as a feeble excuse. In truth, I'd spent the previous three years convincing myself I'd only joined the gang because I had no choice. But in reality, it had become my life by this time.

There was also another reason I had for staying in the drugs trade that I didn't admit to my best friend that night. Though I didn't want to confront the fact, I knew in my heart of hearts that my boss wouldn't just let me walk away from it all. By this time, I knew so much about the gang that he'd have probably felt obliged to do something bad if I turned my back on him.

It should have felt strange to think that way about someone whom I'd grown to trust and respect on so many levels. But I'd already accepted there was a cold hard reality about being a professional criminal, and I now fully appreciated that this was one of the rules of the game. So I made it clear to my old school friend that I didn't want to leave Ibiza, and would not be joining him in London.

At the airport before my friend flew off, he asked me about my boss and how I had come to work for him, and I told him the entire story for the first time. Before leaving me, he warned me to be very careful, as he was convinced that my boss had some ulterior motive for wanting to keep me in the gang. We said goodbye and he left without saying any more about it.

I'd got so used to the Brit by this stage that I'd stopped noticing the obvious signs that he was still searching for something much more substantial than a load of missing drugs. He studied me closely across restaurant tables or whenever we were in the car together. The longer I was in the gang, the more I dismissed it as just my imagination playing tricks with me, so I never confronted him about it. Now, I wasn't sure.

But then again, the Brit was providing me with more of a genuine sense of security than I'd experienced throughout most of my childhood. I was so grateful I didn't want to question his motives in keeping me in the gang. I trusted him so much by this time that when we met one day in a bar in the Old Town to discuss the business, I told him how my best friend had tried to get me to quit. He laughed and invited me to his home for dinner that night with his wife and children. No one else in the gang had even met them, so I felt quite honoured.

His villa turned out to be much less opulent than I expected. As he showed me around it, he explained that he preferred to live modestly and that his wife and children had no idea what he did for a living. This helped ensure his family remained grounded and also helped him avoid any enquiries by inquisitive cops. So it was no surprise when the Brit introduced me to his wife as his "marketing assistant". He even spent 10 minutes chatting to me in front of her about the furniture and kitchen equipment import and export market, while occasionally winking in my direction.

I felt very aware that this overlap between our professional and personal lives was unusual within the tight structure of the gang, which seemed to have been built around the presumption that you could not rely on 100 per cent trust between members. I think my boss felt sorry for me because I'd had to continue to live at my mother's villa to keep a closer eye on her. Her alcoholism at this time was worsening further still.

I felt I needed to be there for my mother, even though it was quite a burden. I'd made sure to retain the rented villa on the other side of the Old Town that I'd lent to my father, so I could occasionally escape there with a girlfriend. It was lucky I'd chosen to stay at my mother's villa because she started getting into the habit of wandering out late at night to buy a bottle of gin from the nearest bar, which happened to be more than two miles away. She'd sometimes drink the entire bottle while hobbling home on a stick and then be found unconscious in a ditch the following morning. On other occasions, the Guardia Civil picked her up wandering drunkenly around town and then unceremoniously dumped her on the doorstep of the villa, along with her walking stick that was thrown onto the ground beside her.

I unloaded all this to my boss and his wife that night at his house. It turned out he'd had similar problems with his own elderly mother. They recommended a local woman, who could work as a carer for my mother when I wasn't at the villa. I was deeply touched by their help and left that dinner on a high, grateful that they hadn't minded me confiding in them.

* * *

Back at work the power and influence of the gang continued to grow as Ibiza was fast gaining a reputation as a hedonistic playground during the late 1970s and early 1980s. My boss was immensely proud to have developed the island into a vital hub for the transportation of cannabis across Europe, as well as supplying all Ibiza's pot. As long as the old chief remained in charge, it was fairly easy to get cannabis on and off the island. My boss continued to pay him to keep us informed of any police activities on Ibiza and the mainland that might impact on our operation.

By the early 1980s, I'd been earning big money for some years, and I'd amassed large sums of cash that I didn't really know what to do with. I'd stashed hundreds of thousands of pounds worth of pesetas in a secret hiding place behind my mother's villa. I knew it would only be a matter of time before it was either discovered or lost its value due to the inflation that was running rampant through Spain's economy at the time.

So, as usual, I turned to my boss for advice. He told me that I was right and it was far too risky to leave money in stash holes and that I needed to clean my money through legitimate investments before it lost its value.

Bank accounts were a non-starter, even back then. In Spain, financial authorities were under pressure to report any cash deposits of more than US$5,000. This followed an invasion of Spain in the late 1970s by criminals – often British ones – who couldn't be extradited back to their home countries because there were no such treaties between Spain and other European nations at the time.

In London, my father was incurring yet more gambling debts. I was irritated when he called for help because I'd already paid off those earlier debts. But it sounded much heavier this time. Criminals were regularly knocking on his door in London and threatening him and his girlfriend with physical harm. London was actually in the middle of a property boom, so I decided to send couriers over with suitcases filled with cash from Ibiza to help my father, and also do some dabbling in the city's lucrative house market. My father agreed that in exchange for paying off his debts, he'd purchase properties on my behalf. These could then be turned around for a healthy profit within a couple of years of each deal. It was the perfect way to clean my dirty money and help save my father's life at the same time.

I approached my best friend from school – who was now a fully qualified lawyer – to do the conveyancing on each property. I wanted to ensure we kept certain details secret and to avoid any problems with the UK financial authorities. My friend immediately agreed to do the conveyancing work, and I was surprised about this (given his aversion to my line of work) until he admitted that his wealthy father, the president of the DRWA, had cut him off financially after they fell out.

I was becoming needed. People around me required my support and I liked being able to help them.

CHAPTER TEN
LOST LOVE

I liked to think I was – as they used to say in Ibiza – fully "in the groove" when it came to the drug business by the early 1980s. My work included picking up cannabis from deserted beaches at the dead of night and testing hash to make sure it hadn't been secretly cut by our suppliers in Morocco. They often pulled all sorts of tricks to try and "stretch" out the product. Their favourite method was to add the crushed leaves of green plants, which were then used to expand the load buy as much as twice its natural size. That meant double their profits.

My boss remained my mentor in many ways, despite the years I'd now been a member of his gang. He was always banging on to me about making sure I trusted no one. I still found this hard to do because it was the exact opposite of my natural instincts. When I responded this way yet again to the Brit one evening as we drove to a meeting on the west side of Ibiza, he laughed and accused me of sounding like a stuck record. Our hosts that evening were to be fishermen, who often transported our produce to the mainland.

That evening in the car, the Brit playfully accused me of being in denial about what we did for a living but had the decency to add that if that worked for me than he had no problem with it. I enjoyed reminding him yet again that my inbuilt optimism came from my feral, hippy upbringing.

I was thinking – albeit reluctantly – that maybe I was deluded to use that old chestnut of an excuse, when we were waved down by two men with shotguns slung over their shoulders on a deserted, pitch-black stretch of track running along the island's craggy, northern coastline.

The Brit immediately pulled out his gun but held it out of sight under the front seat as I stopped the car. The two men seemed friendly enough and explained they were out night hunting and wanted to know if we'd spotted any hogs while driving through nearby woodland. But I noticed my boss continued to clutch his gun under the front seat.

After a brief conversation with both men, I fired up the car and we pulled off. The Brit checked behind us every now and again to make sure they were not following. Before we arrived for our meeting with the fishermen, the Brit told me he thought that the men who'd stopped us were connected to them and that they were checking us out in case we were undercover police or other criminals. It was a timely reminder of the world we inhabited.

* * *

What little time off I had from the gang was mainly spent playing guitar with a local band in bars in the Old Town, as well as at the New Zealander's secret beach, which we did on Sunday lunchtimes. Two afternoons a week, the band rehearsed at a hotel owned by the Brit, who by this time had a couple of local businesses to help launder the proceeds of his drug business. It had a nightclub in the basement with a stage and superb acoustics. The Brit said he didn't mind us playing there as long as we were out by early evening.

During the first practice session at the club, more than a dozen girls staying in accommodation above the premises turned up to watch us. It was only then I realized that the club and hotel was actually a brothel. I suppose I was a bit surprised that the Brit boss hadn't told me, but he had a front man running the business, so few knew he was the real owner. In any case, such establishments were not illegal in Spain, as long as they operated as "hotels" and each girl paid a fee for a room. All of the women working there were from South and Central America, the Spanish mainland and Morocco. They would watch and applaud the tracks they liked the best, so it became a good way to test out our performance levels.

One afternoon, I got talking to a Chilean girl who worked in the club. We shared a beer at the bar before the manager walked in and ordered her to get back to "work" because a bunch of Guardia Civil officers in uniform had just appeared in the main bar looking for female company. The following day, I met the same girl for a coffee. She seemed surprised I had no problem with what she did for a living. But with a job like mine, I didn't feel it was my right to judge anyone.

She'd been to university in the Chilean capital Santiago and her family had lost everything following the downfall of left-wing President Allende in a bloody army coup in 1973. This had resulted in the reign of the much-feared General Pinochet, one of Franco's last fascist allies on the globe. She'd come to Ibiza to work as a cleaning lady but was so badly treated and poorly paid by her employer that she'd turned to working as a prostitute. It earned her much more cash to send back to her family in Chile.

I was immediately attracted to her because she was so open about her life. She told me how her brother had been kidnapped by Pinochet's secret police and never seen again. But there was no self-pity about what she told me, and I liked the way she said that one day her family would get revenge on Pinochet, however long it took until he was toppled. She had ambitions to return to Chile and start a business but accepted that in order to raise the money she'd have to work as a prostitute for at least two or three years.

We talked about everything from my mother's civil war adventures to her funny and sad experiences in the brothel. She said her parents were so strong and patient that they'd taught her that the good and bad stuff in life was something to learn from and even cherish. The over-riding message from her was that there was no room for regret. She had an inner calmness, despite everything she'd been through, and that made her even more attractive to me.

Initially, we went out on some dates in the mornings because of her "night work" and visited the secret beach together. The New Zealander knew what she did for a living but never once mentioned it. She told me he'd actually visited the brothel on a number of occasions.

* * *

I was delighted a few weeks later when the Chilean girl got a rare night off from the brothel and I took her out to a local restaurant for dinner. She'd never been out anywhere in Ibiza socially before and was nervous that she might see men who frequented the brothel. I explained to her that it wasn't her problem. They were the ones who'd find it awkward.

That night we bumped into a couple of other members of my gang in a local bar and sat down for a few drinks together before all heading to a nearby nightclub. She seemed very coy in front of the others, but I put that down to her not being used to going on a proper night out. The two gang members with us did seem a bit wary of her, though.

At the nightclub, I started dancing with the Chilean girl and immediately noticed one of the other gang members sniggering at us. When I confronted him, he laughed in my face while pointing out what she did for a job. I accused him of disrespecting her, but he said I needed to get my head round a few "facts" about her. The gang member told me they'd paid her to sleep with me on our first date because they thought I'd appreciate it.

I was so upset, I grabbed my girlfriend by the hand and marched her straight out of the nightclub. I wasn't used to being treated this way by anyone. I'd never slept with a prostitute and had no interest in doing so. It felt very confusing to know she'd been paid to have sex with me after we'd opened up so much to each other. I confronted her in the street outside the nightclub and she insisted that after our first time together, she'd genuinely fallen for me. So I challenged her to quit working as a prostitute and said I'd find her a straight job. She immediately agreed and I felt we had a chance of a proper relationship.

But the following evening I arrived at the brothel to pick her up to find she'd walked out earlier that day, without leaving a forwarding address. I wanted to ask the manager of the hotel where she'd gone, but I knew that would get back to the gang and my boss, so I said nothing. I was completely thrown by her disappearance because I'd had such high hopes for our relationship.

Some days later, I bumped into her in the middle of Ibiza Old Town. She seemed very embarrassed by what had happened between us and kept glancing around to see if anyone was watching us together as we spoke in the street.

After much persuasion, she reluctantly agreed to have a drink with me. I found it hard to believe how close we'd been just a few days earlier. She said she'd stood me up because she felt awkward that my boss – not those two other gang members – had paid her to sleep with me. She also revealed that the day after that first time, my boss met with her to find out what I'd talked about with her. She hadn't liked the way he'd interrogated her because she felt bad about it all by then.

I was completely thrown by all this. I'd learned to trust and respect the Brit, in many ways. Now I felt uncomfortable about my membership of the gang for the first time in years. I presumed he'd been trying to find out if I'd talked openly about the drug business, but that didn't give him the right to interfere with my personal life. At first, I wanted to confront him about what had happened, but then it dawned on me that I couldn't even be certain she was telling the truth, so I gave him the benefit of the doubt and ignored what she'd told me. In any case, she then disappeared again.

A week later, I was helping unload a shipment of cannabis from an inflatable with two other gang members when one of them let slip that the Chilean girl had been recruited as a drug mule for us and that my boss had ordered the others not to tell me, in case it upset me. This changed everything, and I spent the following two or three days trying to track her down but to no avail. She seemed to have disappeared into thin air. But

I did pick up rumours she'd been caught smuggling drugs and arrested on the mainland. It sounded as if she'd agreed to help the police in exchange for her freedom, and that meant there could now be a price on her head, which worried me.

This time I had to make sure I went through with actually confronting my boss, but I kept preparing to do it and then backing down before I saw him. What if everything I'd been told was untrue? Then I'd upset him and possibly even be thrown out of the gang, which could be extremely dangerous for me.

But I still couldn't let go of it, so after I'd picked my Brit boss up from his house one morning, I decided to finally throw caution to the wind. But, typically, he picked up on my distracted mood before I'd even had a chance to speak.

"What's wrong with you?" he asked me, moments after getting in the car.

"Nothing."

"It's that bird, isn't it?" he said.

"Is she working as a mule for you?" I asked.

"Of course she fuckin' is," he said. "Why? What's it to you?"

"It's just that…"

"You need to get real about all this," he said, interrupting me. "Working as a mule is a lot easier than working in the club. She needed money for her family. End of story."

"But surely…"

"Just step away from it, son. It's none of your fuckin' business."

A tense few seconds of silence followed between us.

"Look I get it. I really do," he finally said. "My missus worked in a club in London when I first met her. These sorts of girls go through a lot of shit. But you need to let this one go."

I didn't know whether to believe him or not, but none of that was an excuse for paying the girl to sleep with me because he wanted to know what I'd been saying behind his back. Most troubling of all, I'd thought we were still close friends. What a chump I was. It was another stark reminder of the rules of the underworld that would always exist between us.

I never heard anything more from the Chilean girl and decided to take my boss's advice and concentrate on work. But it was hard to get her out of my head. I couldn't accept that I'd been wrong about her and still hoped that one day I'd meet her again and we'd hook up properly.

Shortly after that, he asked me to run the boats between Ibiza and Tangiers, which picked up all our cannabis produced in the lawless bandit country of Morocco's Atlas Mountains. He even checked with me to make sure I felt okay doing this after what I'd been through when my uncle drowned. I'd avoided boat travel a lot since then, and he clearly noticed.

It certainly brought back memories of that drunken lunch party on the beach. The chief turning up. How my uncle ignored the storm and gave me the only life jacket on board his MTB. And also, how frequently my boss asked me if my uncle had stopped anywhere after leaving the beach that evening or earlier on the day he drowned. No matter how close I got to my boss, I could never quite ask him where this fascination with my uncle's whereabouts came from.

Anyway, the extra cannabis shipments we smuggled on those boats from Morocco's Atlas Mountains up to Ibiza proved to be an incredible money spinner. Demand for pot in Ibiza and mainland Spain and the rest of Europe had shot up during the mid-1980s and loads that now cost £20,000 in Morocco could be turned into a profit of more than £250,000 by handling all the transport and distribution for each shipment.

By this time our cannabis boats were arriving on deserted Ibiza beaches at night from north Africa at least twice a week. The product was then transported by truck to rented houses nearby where it was stored before being reduced in size and repackaged at our warehouse base. The cannabis was usually then shipped out on different vessels heading to the Spanish mainland, where it was picked up and distributed to the rest of Europe and the UK.

It seemed as if the gang could continue running smoothly and making money forever, even despite the occasional presence of America's Drug Enforcement Authority (DEA) agents in North Africa. They were trying to get the Moroccan government to cut the Atlas Mountains off, so that the cannabis industry in Morocco effectively "dried up". It was a naïve plan by the Americans, as the region – roughly the same size as Wales – was dependent on the cannabis industry to employ tens of thousands of locals. So, as a result, the Moroccan authorities always turned a blind eye, and the trade could keep on rolling. But as the profits from the cannabis business soared, so did the threat of violence from those inside the underworld, especially in North Africa.

On one occasion, I arranged to meet a local handler with a tame customs officer in the Moroccan port of Tangiers, and just minutes before they were due to arrive, two of the gangsters supposed to be protecting us were shot dead in the car park in front of the hotel where we were meeting. We managed to get out through a back entrance, but I realized once again that my own obsession with avoiding violence meant nothing to the people I was dealing with.

After years of being told by my boss that the cannabis underworld would never explode into violence as the cocaine business had, I'd been exposed to professional criminals who wouldn't hesitate to kill rivals if they thought they were being ripped off or were police informants. I was expressly banned by my boss from admitting to other criminals that I refused to ever carry a gun, because he saw this as a weakness, which might one day cost us dearly.

In Morocco we eventually decided to partner up with a warlord in the Atlas Mountains because he had direct connections with the Moroccan royal family. This would further help guarantee that our cannabis had a safe passage out of the country, despite the DEA and other law enforcement agencies. Warlords had taken over much of the cannabis business in the notoriously lawless Atlas Mountains area. Each one controlled his own territory, which tended to be at least the size of the whole of Ibiza.

Over on the other side of the Atlantic, America's obsession with breaking up supply routes for cannabis and cocaine coming from South and Central America meant that Mexico was emerging as the safest transport hub. Its entire infrastructure revolved around wholesale police corruption, and drugs could be effectively shipped through there to just about anywhere in the world. Mexican mafia gangs across the nation were running their own cartels to handle all the drugs coming through their country. This meant the price of cannabis from Latin America was double what we were paying in Morocco. We were carefully monitoring that marketplace just in case the DEA ever effectively impacted the cannabis business in Morocco. But for the time being, our twice-a-week shipments from the Atlas Mountains were evolving into a conveyor belt of cannabis that had the potential to bring in millions of pounds every year to the gang, as long as we could maintain reasonable relations with our tame warlord.

My trips abroad gave me a reputation among the other members of the gang as someone happy to handle the foreign end of the business. Most professional criminals loathe this side of the job because they feel vulnerable away from their home territory, but having no strong sense of home, I didn't mind.

I was even sent by my boss to negotiate cannabis deals with Corsica's notorious mafia. The French-run island across the Mediterranean from Ibiza had a reputation as a self-run criminal state within a state. One time, one of its mob bosses announced that he wanted to quadruple the size of the monthly shipment of cannabis we'd been supplying to his gang up until then. My boss smelt a rat, so I was sent over to investigate. I travelled by light plane across to Corsica feeling quite apprehensive because the island's gangsters were notoriously trigger-happy and I was about to enter their territory alone.

I was picked up at a tiny airfield on the island by two henchmen who couldn't speak English or Spanish and my French wasn't good, so we travelled in complete silence to a huge mountainside villa to meet the main man. At the house, his two goons insisted on searching me, despite having already done so once at the airfield. It felt intimidatory, as if they were trying to test me. Someone without my patience might have lost it with them, but getting antsy wasn't in my DNA.

The main boss appeared just as I was putting my trousers back on. He seemed amused by what had just happened and clapped me on the back. Then – in broken English – he told me to join him in an adjoining room. I walked in to find a long dining room table with four place settings. Already sitting at two of them were two women in their mid-twenties. He insisted we had dinner with them before discussing the deal. The women were prostitutes hired for the evening. Luckily one of them spoke English, so I was able to converse with her, but there were a lot of awkward silences and I couldn't understand why he'd insisted on having them there in the first place.

After the main course, the Corsican boss leaned across one of the women sitting between us and said she would be waiting for me after our meeting. Then he stood up and we retired to another adjoining room. The Corsican immediately demanded a 30 per cent reduction on our usual price for cannabis because it was four times the size of the usual shipments. Before I'd left Ibiza, the Brit had warned me not to do any cut-price deals with the Corsicans because he didn't want them to start trying to pay less for every subsequent load. That had put a lot of pressure on me. But there was a danger I wouldn't get out of there alive if I didn't do some kind of deal. So we eventually settled on a halfway agreement, which meant a 15 per cent discount on condition I was taken straight to the airfield that night because, I told him, I had an urgent appointment to keep back in Ibiza.

It was a risky, almost naïve strategy on my part because I was going against my boss's express orders. But I had no intention of staying at the Corsican's villa or sleeping with one of his call girls. I stressed about this decision nonstop during the flight back to Ibiza. It felt as if my boss had deliberately put me in danger. I hated the way that paranoia was now part and parcel of my mindset.

By the time I met up with the Brit the morning after I got back to Ibiza, I was completely wound up. However, within moments of sitting down with him in his office at the furniture warehouse, he'd admitted building 15 per cent "padding" into the Corsican deal knowing full well that they would make such demands. Inside I was seething. I couldn't understand why he hadn't told me all this before I went to Corsica. But instead of confronting him, I just let it slide. I never really got to the bottom of what he was playing at. But things were starting to happen between us which made me feel that I needed to start watching my back at all times.

My boss ended up paying me a hefty bonus for securing the Corsican deal. I think he actually felt a bit bad about putting my head on the block like that. At least the extra cash enabled me to send over enough money for my father to purchase some new properties in the centre of London.

On Ibiza, I continued to stick rigidly to my own non-violence pledge in the hope we'd always try to find peaceful solutions rather than resorting to violence, despite the occasional "incident". When one gang member asked for permission to kill one of our transport agents because a large amount of cash had gone missing, I persuaded my boss to allow me to investigate what had happened before any violent measures were taken. I'd already worked out by this time that most professional criminals don't really want to hear the truth unless it is their version of the truth. They are masters at twisting the facts to their own advantage, and that's often when things turn deadly.

I eventually got both men in this dispute around a table to discuss the missing cash and we talked through it carefully. In the end, it turned out to have all been a huge misunderstanding because the cash had been deposited in the wrong money-launderer's bank account. After this potential bloodbath was avoided, my boss started calling me "the diplomat". The nickname had quite a calming effect on many of our criminal associates because they'd always ask why I was called that, and once it was explained, they seemed strangely reassured.

CHAPTER ELEVEN
CUBAN CROSSING

One day, the New Zealander turned up at my mother's villa to see how she was, though I think it was just an excuse to warn me to step back from the drug business. When I pointed out that I only dealt in cannabis and it was no more harmful than alcohol, he laughed and said: "That's what they all say." He was convinced that once all the old Franco cronies were finally driven out of Ibiza then my days as a drug lord would be numbered. He sounded genuinely worried for me, so I thanked him for his concern.

It was the late 1980s and the Brit and the rest of us thought we were pretty invincible when it came to Ibiza's cannabis business by this time. Despite those recent incidents, we still believed we could continue to see off all our rivals, usually without even resorting to violence.

I still worked on the basis of good karma and zen-like philosophies, especially when it came to our role in the cannabis trade. We were the good guys of the drug trade, after all. I even managed to persuade my boss not to retaliate against two cannabis gangsters operating from the Spanish mainland whom he suspected of stealing one of our loads of drugs when it was en route to the island. I convinced him that any violence would spark a bloody war that we'd probably lose because this rival gang was ten times the size of us.

But I could tell he was growing weary of my pacifist attitude. One day, he said that my naïvity made us more vulnerable and that the drug underworld was turning into a multi-billion-dollar business, which meant the rules were changing. I ignored my boss's cynicism and continued going out of my way to smile at all the Guardia Civil officers I encountered in Ibiza, knowing full well that many of them hated my guts because they knew I was working in the drug business.

My problems at home were much more immediate, though. My sickly mother now had a full-time carer because she'd become even more seriously depleted by her dependency on alcohol and tranquilizers. One evening, I got back to the villa from a trip to Morocco to find her unconscious on the floor, lying in a pool of her own urine. Her carer had walked out a few hours earlier and my mother's wallet containing tens of thousands of pesetas was missing.

I cleaned my mother up and carried her to bed, leaving her to sleep it all off. Then I called my boss and poured out everything about my mother. After he'd listened carefully to what had happened, he said it was clear my mother had never got over my uncle's drowning. I remember wondering at that moment why he was still so obsessed with the fallout from that fateful evening all those years later, and I spent the night with that concern in the back of my mind.

The following morning, I made breakfast for my mother and sat on the end of her bed to make sure she ate it all for a change. She asked me if I was still working for the Brit. I reluctantly nodded. Then she turned over onto one side of her bed and closed her eyes tightly. I knew there was no point in asking why she'd brought it up.

* * *

While my home life fell apart, the cannabis business continued to go from strength to strength. In 1988, we purchased a much bigger warehouse on the edge of Ibiza Old Town where we could repackage the cannabis and sell it off in much smaller loads that were easier to transport and far more profitable. We had another smaller lock-up garage well away from the main warehouse because we were dealing in such huge quantities of cash that we kept bank note machines in a secure building where we counted it all.

At least 10 per cent of all our income went into the pockets of corrupt public officials. My boss continued paying the same old Guardia Civil chief, who'd somehow clung on to his job in Ibiza, despite fresh purges of Franco's law enforcement cronies across the rest of Spain. One time, I drove past a restaurant and saw my boss and the chief – now in his mid-seventies – eating a meal together. I found it hard to watch after all the stuff that had happened in the past involving the chief. But I'd learned to accept that it was part of my boss's job to pay off anyone who helped our corporation, as we now considered ourselves.

In many ways, the gang I belonged to in Ibiza was nothing more than a medium-sized cog in a huge piece of illicit machinery. Sticking to only dealing in cannabis seemed old fashioned, but I never complained because everyone knew the risks would be much greater if we moved into the cocaine trade.

Some potential problems began emerging on Ibiza itself, though. Our monopoly of the cannabis business had inevitably alerted other criminals to the "market potential" of the island. One emerging young gangster was a Cuban I'd known during my childhood on Ibiza. His family had moved to the island in the late 1950s after communist revolutionary Fidel Castro took over his homeland and Franco offered the hand of friendship to any families with Spanish ancestry wanting to move back to their motherland.

This same Cuban had opened his own small-scale cannabis business without bothering to come and ask us permission. We'd heard he was paying mules to bring the drugs over from the mainland, so it was a relatively small set-up; however, my boss wanted to stop the Cuban in his tracks before he got too big for his boots. As usual, I urged him not to take the violent route in order to avoid a war, although on this occasion we would be certain to win it. To make matters worse, my boss had met the Cuban socially because his children were friends with his. He said he hated those type of crossovers and it made him even more determined to stop the Cuban in his tracks.

In the end, we sat down with the Cuban and agreed that he could supply the second-largest town on the island, San Antonio, through its bars and clubs. But he would have to buy all his cannabis through us, and the rest of the island remained our exclusive territory. The agreement would only make a small dent in our earnings, as we'd be making money from selling him the drugs. In any case, the majority of our income by this time came from exporting cannabis to the UK and mainland Europe through our carefully controlled transportation routes.

Our costs had begun going up because we were having to pay out so many more bribes to the police and customs. This wasn't just in Ibiza but also Valencia and Barcelona and half a dozen other ports on the Spanish mainland, which we regularly used.

At first, the arrangement with the Cuban worked out well. Then, after about nine or ten months, we got word that he'd approached a Chilean cocaine cartel and was trying to secure an exclusive deal to buy their cocaine and sell it in Ibiza. As we all knew, dealing in cocaine was a different ballgame altogether. The profits were five – maybe even ten – times higher, but the risks to one's health and liberty were much more when compared to dealing in cannabis. Also, prison sentences were three times longer and murder had become an almost daily occurrence inside the cocaine underworld.

We heard from an informant inside the Cuban's gang that he was trying to persuade the Chileans to smuggle their cocaine through a specific Mexican drug transportation cartel before it came across to Europe. This seemed very strange, so we investigated further and discovered that the Mexicans had deliberately encouraged the Cuban to deal with the Chilean cartel. They wanted to handle the transportation of all their cocaine going to Europe, which was fast turning into the most lucrative drugs market in the world after the United States.

Initially, we held back to see how things evolved between the Cuban, the Chilean cartel and the Mexicans. It was the end of the 1980s and the drugs marketplace had transformed since US President Ronald Reagan's much-publicized War on Drugs a few years earlier. This had led to a notable increase in demand for both cannabis and cocaine in Europe and the UK, so we were considering whether we needed to move with the times and start also dealing in cocaine.

That was when it all turned nasty. One night, one of our street dealers in the north of Ibiza was kidnapped by members of the Cuban's gang. Our man was tortured because they wanted to know more about how our operation worked. They killed him in the end because he told them nothing, and his death was one of the first blatant drugs-underworld-related murders on the island.

The chief – who'd been there when my uncle had drowned – warned my boss that unless we retained control of the island's drugs trade and everything calmed down, a specialized police anti-drug unit based in Madrid would come to Ibiza to forcibly break up the island's narcotics underworld, which the media were claiming was out of control. The chief also warned my boss that despite all the bribes he'd received down the years, he'd be powerless to stop that Madrid unit from coming to Ibiza once that decision was made. We had a couple of weeks at the most to straighten things out.

You could say we had no choice but to enter the cocaine business then. My boss arranged for us to go to Madrid immediately to meet the Chilean cartel's Spanish representative to hammer out a deal to guarantee we had exclusive rights to all their shipments of cocaine coming into Europe. We were informed by the Chileans that we would be meeting a woman known as "La Patrona", which translates as "the landlady" but essentially meant she was in charge. She was running their operation in Madrid and was renowned for being a tough negotiator.

* * *

My Brit boss seemed a bit down as we flew out to the Spanish capital the following morning. He said he hated these types of meetings because they could be so unpredictable and if we did anything to piss off the Chileans they'd probably kill us there and then. It didn't exactly fill me with confidence. But instead of getting nervous, I went into one of my classic zen-like states and tried to look at the positive side of things, although it wasn't easy. We were literally stepping into the lion's den, and we didn't really know how it would all pan out.

We travelled by taxi from Madrid Airport to a hotel on the south side of the city to be met by two men in the reception area, who took us straight up to a penthouse suite to meet La Patrona. After a half-hour wait in the suite, she finally walked in.

I thought I was seeing things. My boss kicked me in the shin so I didn't say anything. La Patrona was the Chilean prostitute I thought I'd once been in love with five years earlier. She was accompanied by two henchmen, who'd no doubt report everything they saw and heard back to their cartel bosses in Chile.

For the following hour, we conducted a meeting with her without once referring to our previous "connections". She was dressed like the head of a corporation, in a tight-fitting dress, heels and pristine make-up. There was no sign of the tattoos she'd had on her hand and the side of her neck when I'd known her.

By the end of the meeting, we'd agreed to pay 10 per cent more than the Cuban had offered for the Chilean cartel's cocaine, on condition the cartel covered the costs of transporting their product from Mexico to Galicia in northern Spain via local fishing fleets. We'd handle its onward journey to Ibiza.

Even as we shook hands on the deal, no reference was made to our previous connection. In many ways, it was a relief, because there were so many questions to ask her that it would have undoubtedly endangered our agreement and been reported straight back to her cartel boss in Chile. It wasn't until we got in the lift of the hotel that my boss and I acknowledged to each other who she was. He warned me not to be tempted to contact her because the cartel would definitely come after us if they knew about my involvement with her.

At about 2 a.m. the following morning, I got a call in my hotel room from her. I should have put the phone down immediately, but her voice sounded completely different from earlier. It was much softer, more hesitant and vulnerable. She apologized about not acknowledging me and said she really missed me.

I didn't answer her at first because I feared it might be a trap to see if I would ever talk about our relationship. She sounded disappointed when I didn't respond but then repeated how much she'd missed me. I had no doubt from the tone of her voice that she meant it. So when she asked me to visit her apartment, I agreed.

An hour later we were in bed together. I knew it was a mistake to sleep with her, but I couldn't really help myself. I'd thrown all my boss's advice out of the window in a moment of madness. But it didn't feel wrong to be with her and that made it all even more confusing.

CHAPTER TWELVE
LA PATRONA

That night she told me everything. How she'd operated as a mule for our gang and got similar work for the Chilean cartel through a friend of her family. She'd almost died when a bag of cocaine split in her stomach during one smuggling run from Santiago to Madrid. The Chilean cartel boss had been in Madrid at the time and paid for her to be treated in a private hospital, as well as buying off the Spanish police to drop the charges against her following her arrest at the airport after collapsing.

Once she got out of hospital, the Chilean cartel boss expected her to repay his kindness and they slept together. After that, he set her up in a big apartment as his mistress, and nine months later they had a baby together. The cartel boss gave her the job of running the cartel's business in Spain on condition she remained his Madrid-based lover.

She told me that she hated him because she knew he would have her killed if he ever thought she might spill any of the cartel's secrets, but their baby son had been born disabled and he'd paid for all his medical treatment. She said that the child was the most important person in her life and that she would do anything for him.

She admitted she'd deliberately manipulated the situation with the Cuban in the hope we'd come to her for cocaine, as she wanted us to meet again. I was delighted, but also terrified. The cartel boss was no man to be messed with. Before I left her apartment that morning, she insisted I didn't tell anyone – not even my boss – that we'd slept together.

"I promise I won't," I said before letting myself out of her apartment and heading down the hallway towards the elevators.

The lift door opened before I reached it, and a smartly dressed brunette woman in her early twenties stepped out. She gave me a knowing glance as I passed her in the hallway. I smiled back just as the elevator doors closed before I could reach them.

Then – while waiting for the next lift to arrive – I noticed the woman letting herself into La Patrona's apartment with a key at the other end of the hallway.

* * *

I shared a taxi to the airport with my boss later that morning. He seemed very preoccupied and kept studying me closely, which quite unnerved me. Then he asked me if I had anything to tell him.

"No. Nothing. Why?" I asked.

"Well," he replied. "You weren't in your room last night when I called about the flight times changing."

I insisted I must have slept through his call and had been in bed the entire time, though I knew he didn't believe me.

He again warned me to stay away from La Patrona. The previous day he'd sounded more like a father with his son than a crime boss, but this time his tone had hardened.

"We're in the cocaine business now," he said, under his breath so the cab driver couldn't hear him. "It's a different ballgame, son. Put a foot wrong and we're both fucked."

Despite his warning, the moment I got back to Ibiza, I called La Patrona. She sounded coldly detached. I could hear another woman's voice in the background asking her who she was speaking to. Then she told me not to call her ever again.

La Patrona ignored a dozen more of my calls over the following couple of days and then left a blunt message on my answering machine telling me to stop calling, saying, "it's over". I knew only too well that if I told anyone else what had happened between us then it was going to cost people's lives, so I stopped trying to contact her.

I never mentioned my feelings for La Patrona to the Brit. The deal for the cocaine shipments we'd agreed in Madrid went ahead as planned and I kept to my promise to keep away from her. But I never forgot her.

* * *

There were a lot of advantages to dealing in cocaine, the main one being the size of it compared to cannabis. It was a revelation to us at first as we found that we could transport millions of pounds worth of cocaine in a suitcase.

It could also be wrapped in airtight plastic and hidden in lobster pots submerged and tied to special lines, which were marked with buoys. The most popular spot for these drop-offs was the bay near the rice fields in Ibiza, as the sea was so shallow that law enforcement couldn't properly patrol in their new power boats.

The Brit employed a retired chemist in his early seventies from the north of the island to help us come up with new ways to transport cocaine without risking damage to the product. Despite his age, he was completely unfazed by the serious criminal implications of what he was doing with us.

He told me once he loved the challenge of working out ingenious ways to "melt" cocaine in such a way that whoever received it at the other end would be able to convert it back into the "real thing". One of his cleverest inventions was cocaine jeans. These were actually denim jeans that were soaked in liquid cocaine and then dried and stacked on top of each other, complete with store labels that were put back on the jeans once they'd been dried out.

The chemist painstakingly showed us how you could use a hot iron to carefully heat up the denim and then fold each pair into a tiny, tight-fitting bundle which would cause the cocaine to harden and then crack enough to remove in slabs from the inside lining of the jeans. My boss was so pleased that he took us all out for dinner, and we toasted the chemist at least a dozen times during the meal, much to his embarrassment. He got totally wasted and had to be dropped home on his doorstep, much to the disgust of his elderly wife.

The biggest difference between cocaine and cannabis, though, was that cocaine could be cut much more easily. This meant we could increase our profits by a further 10 times. We always tried to ensure the product still contained about 35 per cent actual cocaine, to be certain of hooking in the customers, but the rest was fair game. Once it had been cut, we'd distribute 25 per cent of it across the island and ship the other 75 per cent to the mainland and beyond. This was done as quickly as possible, as keeping it stored in one place remained very risky, even though it was much smaller and easier to handle than cannabis.

Up until this time, all I knew about the cartel – apart from La Patrona – was that it was based in Santiago, Chile. The Brit was careful not to tell any of us more details, for our own protection. The less we knew about the cartel itself, the better. My boss was a stickler for what he called "security". He was always banging on about how we were safer dealing with the Chileans than any of the trigger-happy Colombian cartels who dominated the cocaine underworld at that time and still do to this day.

All communications with the Chileans went through La Patrona for months, and everything seemed to go even more smoothly than we had expected. My boss begrudgingly conceded that he should have gone into the cocaine business much sooner.

Then something happened which was a chilling reminder that we were now dealing with a product that was much more deadly than cannabis.

* * *

About six months after we'd signed our agreement with the Chilean cartel, I saw a news report on Spanish TV about a body being found floating in a reservoir south of Madrid. The Spanish media quoted the police saying that they believed the victim had been murdered by a foreign drug gang in the city.

I didn't think much about it until a few days later, when I picked up a Madrid daily newspaper at a news stand in Ibiza Old Town. On the front page was a story stating that the same victim had been a woman running a Chilean cocaine cartel's Madrid cell. I knew immediately it had to be La Patrona. My heart sank and I felt so dizzy that I stopped in the middle of a busy plaza and sat down on a bench while I regained my composure.

The article went on to reveal that the victim had also been the Chilean cartel boss's mistress and that her murder was connected to a gang war between South American cartels. The police also revealed to the newspaper that she had received injuries consistent with having been tortured before her death.

I was due to meet the Brit for a coffee in the nearby old port area just a few minutes later. I sat on that bench for at least 10 minutes just staring into space while I flashed back to every occasion I'd met her. I'd nursed a secret wish that one day we'd get together properly, quit the drug business and then live happily ever after in a perfect world.

Instead, I was on a bench in a busy plaza trying to make sense of her murder. I couldn't bail out of my meeting with the Brit, so 10 minutes later I was sitting down in a crowded, noisy café when he walked around the corner and headed in my direction. He had a copy of the same newspaper I'd read earlier under his arm. I immediately went into a panic. What could I say to him about it? Then I remembered I'd lied to him about seeing her in Madrid, so I couldn't say a thing.

We sat there making light conversation for at least 10 minutes, both equally reluctant to broach the subject of La Patrona. Just when I decided I couldn't hold back any longer, he started speaking.

"Don't go there, son," he said, as if reading my mind. "It's not our problem."

I tried to adopt what I thought was a classic criminal mindset: I knew that now I had to keep all my innermost thoughts to myself. That meant never telling another soul what had happened between me and her. That didn't stop the murder of La Patrona eating away at me, though, and that afternoon, following my meeting with the Brit, I began doing some discrete digging. Within days, I'd established that she'd been killed on the direct orders of the Chilean cartel boss after he'd discovered she had a secret lover.

I started wondering if my boss had told the Chileans about my affair with her. As the days passed, I realized I couldn't let it go, so I decided to confront him. It was undoubtedly a risky move. He would have every right to be upset with me for daring to question his leadership, as well as for having defied his express orders not to see La Patrona. But instead of being angry, the Brit told me to stay calm because he had expressly been informed that the cartel boss had ordered her to be killed because she was considered a "security risk" and that it had nothing to do with me. I was so astonished he was being reasonable that I wondered if he was simply protecting me because I was a useful asset for him. He could see I was worried and immediately made it clear we should drop the subject and never talk about it again.

No one ever came after me about my connection to La Patrona, which meant my boss had kept quiet about that relationship to the cartel, so I started to feel that maybe he had genuinely looked out for me after all. But as the weeks passed following her murder, I did develop a burning hatred towards the Chilean cartel boss. I knew we couldn't just cancel our shipments from him, but I was so distracted by what had happened to La Patrona that I started to lose my grasp on the job at hand. I was angry, but those feelings were tempered by a certain gratitude towards my boss for covering for me.

At home, my now very sickly mother started to ask me what was wrong. She said I was walking around looking glum and preoccupied much of the time. I couldn't get La Patrona out of my head and I felt I had to do something, even though that could put me in great personal danger. After days of trying to avoid opening up to my mother for fear it might make her deteriorating health worse, I broke down and told her about the murder of this woman and the relationship we had. She didn't seem at all surprised, and when I'd finished she told me: "You must do something, or it will haunt you for the rest of your life."

The Brit would have said to completely ignore what happened because any response against the Chilean cartel might provoke a war. But maybe I wasn't really the fully fledged professional criminal I thought I was? There was an anger inside me that I couldn't shake off. Anyone pushed to the limit will eventually snap. So I decided to ignore the most important code in the criminal underworld.

* * *

The following morning, I began discretely researching ways to contact the DEA without implicating myself or the gang. My intention was to give them enough concrete evidence about the Chilean cartel boss to ensure he was arrested. I knew it was in many ways more dangerous than just going out and shooting him, but I convinced myself there was a good karma aspect to doing it this way because he'd end up imprisoned, not murdered.

But when I sat down and properly thought through exactly how I could achieve this goal, my entire plan started to fall apart. It was madness. Any communication with the DEA wasn't worth the risk. Cold-calling the DEA was just about the most stupid thing I could do, and it wouldn't necessarily even result in him being arrested.

So I decided instead to defy all my supposedly peaceful instincts and find a hitman to kill that Chilean cartel leader, but it didn't sit easily with me. I'd spent my entire criminal career convincing other gangsters not to use violence during disputes. Now I was looking for someone to commit the ultimate act of violence – murder.

I even tried to convince myself that this was a separate issue from the usual "gang business" because the murder of a woman I cared for had been very personal for me. But did that really give me the right to do it? Also, I needed to make sure that whoever I approached did not tell anyone I'd commissioned the hit, because I'd be sentenced to death if anyone, including my boss, knew what I'd done.

Despite wrestling with such issues for hours, I still found myself wanting to do it. My mother was right; I'd never get over the heartbreak caused by her death if I didn't avenge it in some way. But finding a hitman isn't easy, even if you work inside the underworld. I wanted as few people as possible to know what I was doing, which meant I needed to tread extremely carefully. I couldn't ask my boss or any of the other gang members because they'd soon work out who my target was. And they were the only people I knew well inside the criminal underworld.

In the end, I got a recommendation from a German drug dealer, who was a former member of the gang. I told him a friend of mine needed to avenge the man who killed his father and promised him a hefty introduction fee on condition he told no one about the proposed hit.

By the time I got his contact details, it was too late at night to phone the hitman there and then, but at least I went to sleep safe in the knowledge that I was on my way to getting justice for the murder of my girlfriend. Then, before I'd even talked to the contract killer, something happened.

CHAPTER THIRTEEN
DEATH AND DESTRUCTION

On a deserted, dusty road just outside the Arturo Merino Benítez International Airport, on the edge of the Chilean capital of Santiago, a paramilitary police unit stopped a fleet of limousines and ordered the occupants out of the vehicles. When half a dozen of those in the cars came out shooting in all directions, the special forces law enforcement unit fired back. In the hail of gunfire, the boss of the Chilean cartel was killed. He'd been planning to board a plane to Madrid using a forged passport, fleeing arrest in his home country.

When I saw the report about it on the evening news, I was stunned. I'd found myself caught up in the middle of a web of violence and retribution after years of managing to avoid it. True, I hadn't actually pulled the trigger, but in many ways I wished I had, and my connection with La Patrona could even make me a suspect in the eyes of the law.

The press in Spain reported that Chilean authorities had been tipped off by the Guardia Civil in Madrid some days before the cartel boss planned to flee Chile. They also mentioned fascist connections between old school Guardia Civil officers in Madrid and the Pinochet right-wing regime in Chile.

Unfortunately, I knew I couldn't confide in the one person in the world who might help me work through these weird feelings of guilt – my boss. If he even so much as suspected I had been planning my own hit on the cartel chief, he'd most likely be obliged to have me killed. That was the law of the underworld jungle: if you inform on anyone – even an enemy – you die. I was sure he wouldn't believe me if I said I hadn't done it.

It came as no big surprise when a few days after the murder, my boss asked me if I'd heard anything about who might have done it. He then used the killing to re-emphasize all his earlier warnings about how much more dangerous the cocaine business was than the cannabis one.

"If you know anything about it, I need to be told," he said. "The Chileans will come back at whoever they think did this, and we could find ourselves in the middle of a bloody war."

At that moment, I had an inkling that he knew who was really behind it. I suspected that the old Guardia Civil chief had told him, but he didn't confide in me because, in his mind at least, I might also be one of the prime suspects linked to the cartel boss's murder.

A few days later, the Chileans sent a two-man team to Ibiza to look into the death of their boss. They'd been tipped off that the person who had informed on the cartel chief's movements was based on the island. We'd already been informed that the cartel had been taken over by his daughter and was still open for business.

The Chilean "investigators" immediately made it clear to the Brit that whoever was responsible would be "taken care of". They openly spoke about how the new cartel boss had demanded revenge for the death of her father. When my boss voiced concern to them that a woman in her twenties was now running the cartel, the Chilean men smiled and said the young woman they referred to as "La Princesa" had even bigger balls than her father. Things were continuing as usual, despite the murder of their boss.

The following morning, I was awoken by the sound of a car pulling up outside my mother's villa. Looking out of the window, I immediately recognized the grim-faced Chileans as they got out of their rental vehicle. I presumed they'd found out about my relationship with La Patrona, so I headed quickly down to the front door before my mother could. Luckily, she was still asleep in her bedroom. I didn't want her to witness what might be about to happen.

I managed to convince the two Chileans that we should chat in their car rather than in the villa because my mother was "sick". Once I'd got in their vehicle, one of them asked how much I knew about La Patrona. I lied and said very little apart from having been introduced to her briefly during that meeting in Madrid.

The older of the two Chileans coldly explained that La Patrona had been tortured by their boss before she'd been killed because he'd wanted to know who her secret lover was.

"She was a brave woman," said the Chilean. "Because she never told him anything and it cost her her life."

He revealed that their investigation on Ibiza had led them to conclude that her lover must have been someone she'd met when she was working as a prostitute on the island. I presumed they were about to point the finger at me, but I tried not to give anything away and just nodded.

"Did you know that one of her clients was the Guardia Civil chief?" one of them asked me.

"Really?" I replied.

"That dirty old man was obsessed with her," said the Chilean. "He wanted our *jefe* (boss) killed because he'd murdered her. So he told the police in Santiago about our *jefe*'s movements and that's how they got to him."

"So it was a crime of passion?" I asked.

The two Chileans looked a bit confused when I said that. In all seriousness, I was still worried that maybe what they'd said was all a trick to see how I responded.

"So what's your next move?" I asked them.

"We have a plan," said the older Chilean, before politely opening the car door and thanking me for my help.

As they drove away, I let myself in through the front door and the telephone rang. It was my boss. He knew I'd been interviewed by the Chileans and asked what they had wanted, but I suspected he already knew the answer to that question.

Later I'd discover how the Brit knew about the Guardia Civil chief and why the chief had to take the rap for something he didn't do.

CHAPTER FOURTEEN
CROSSING THE LINE

The morning after that, the two Chileans caught a flight off the island and the chief's body was found floating in the sea just off the port at Ibiza Old Town close to a local beauty spot. It was so badly mangled up by the propellors of a couple of passing fishing boats that it was impossible to tell how he'd actually died.

There was little surprise and a lot of relief in Ibiza that one of the island's last surviving Franco "warhorses" had finally gone. The list of locals suspected of involvement in his murder was so long that most assumed his killer would never be brought to justice. For the moment, though, no one was openly linking his death to the Chilean cocaine cartel and the murder of its leader on a road near Santiago Airport a few weeks earlier.

The day after the body of the chief was recovered, I was cooking breakfast for my mother while waiting for her latest helper to turn up before I went off to work. The entire front page of the newspaper that morning was a splash about the chief's death. My mother noticed it and immediately picked it up from the table.

After I put a plate of jamon and eggs in front of her, she pushed it aside and carried on reading. When I asked her if she was okay, she ignored me and continued studying the newspaper report. Once she'd finished it, she neatly folded the newspaper and placed it back on the kitchen table where she'd found it without saying another word. I think there was a tear in the corner of her eye but I didn't have the courage to ask her what was wrong.

* * *

My gang continued shipping cocaine from the Chilean cartel, despite the recent killing of their boss. We cranked up our supply chain on Ibiza, swamping the island with cocaine and cannabis, as well as exporting enormous quantities of both drugs to other parts of Europe.

Initially, the death of the police chief was believed by many on the island to be payback for the civil war. The new Policia Nacional chief who replaced him was not even aware his predecessor had been taking bribes from my boss and most probably many others. Luckily the new "liberal" police force seemed far less interested in the drugs scene on the island. I heard rumours that the police had been ordered by the new socialist government in Madrid to allow the narcotics business to thrive, as it would help improve the whole of Spain's economy. As a result, we found it even easier to bring drugs in and out of the island. We were also saving money because we didn't have to pay big bribes to anyone on Ibiza for the first time in 20 years.

However, Ibiza's growing popularity as a holiday island did start to attract some unwanted attention. One British newspaper launched an investigation into the death of the old police chief and published allegations that he'd been in league with a South American cocaine cartel, which had been using Ibiza as a transit point for large cocaine shipments coming across the Atlantic. The paper interviewed the police in Chile, who confirmed that the old chief had actually been the informant who led them to killing the Chilean cartel boss. The same newspaper also alleged that Ibiza was at the centre of a drug turf war first sparked some time earlier by the death of our dealer at the hands of the Cuban's gangsters. I remember asking my boss at that time what had happened to the Cuban. He said it wasn't my problem, and his voice had a nasty edge to it, which made it all sound more personal, so I left it alone.

In this new "liberal" age, our gang continued booming under the stewardship of my boss. Shortly after the new order came into force, he announced that we'd doubled our profits since the days of only handling cannabis. The Brit was so pleased with all my work that he gave me a huge bonus and decided to make me his official deputy. Throughout this profitable period, the gang consisted of a core of 10 men, who worked for us across the island. They organized everything from picking up shipments to handling foreign suppliers to running the teams of street dealers.

As the number of visitors to the island swelled in the middle of the 1990s, so did demand for our drugs. This eventually resulted in more than 50 per cent of all our produce actually being sold directly on the island. The rest continued to be exported through our carefully developed transport routes to the UK and the rest of Europe. But selling on the island was far less risky because we could push the drugs out very quickly and keep the distribution close.

Things were going well in London, too. My father had proved to be a surprisingly astute property speculator by managing to almost triple the cash investments I'd sent over from Ibiza, thanks to some extremely shrewd property deals. His last lot of gambling debts had been completely repaid and it actually felt immensely satisfying to have been able to help him out, despite all the problematic history between us. Times were good.

* * *

One night, my boss and I met up to oversee the arrival of a shipment of bulky Moroccan cannabis being delivered by two inflatables to an isolated beach close to the rice fields. As we waited under a full moon for the arrival of the drugs, my boss mentioned the death of the Chilean cartel chief again and how we had to hope his daughter La Princesa didn't suffer the same fate because that would bring our business crashing down all around us.

After we'd unloaded the cannabis onto a truck, my boss insisted I accompany him in his car while the other two gang members took the flatbed to our warehouse. Inside the car, there was an awkward silence between us. My boss – looking straight ahead into the darkness only illuminated by our headlights – seemed preoccupied by something, and we continued driving without saying a word to each other.

Just before we got to the warehouse, the Brit turned to me and said: "Look, we all wanted that greedy old Guardia Civil chief iced. But if I ever find out you were involved, I won't be able to protect you. D'you understand?"

I tried to explain to him that I played no part in the murder, but he didn't seem to believe me, although he didn't actually say it. I couldn't understand why he'd put this on me. It didn't make sense. It felt as if I was being deliberately blamed for things I hadn't actually done. Was it possible he was trying to pin stuff on me to camouflage his own involvement? If that was the case, then our once close relationship really was in pieces.

All this tension between us also further aided my boss to own me hook, line and sinker in a sense. That meant any aspirations I might have once had about quitting the drug business were about as dead in the water as I would be if I tried to run. For many years before this, it had felt as if I was safe because I had the key to something he wanted, even though I didn't fully know what that was. From that day he accused me of killing the chief, though, I felt I was very much on my own and our relationship had been irreparably damaged.

I'd been naïve all along. The Brit had played me from the moment he picked me up outside the Guardia Civil headquarters after my uncle's MTB sank. Any attempt to change the rules back then would have been tantamount to putting my neck in the noose so I had stuck to the work at hand. On that front, we both knew only too well that if we crossed the South Americans in any way, we'd end up in a shallow grave, so we had to stick together for the moment at least. The risks were much higher now and the way we operated as criminals needed to reflect that.

Meanwhile, in the back of my mind I was becoming increasingly convinced that nearly everything which had happened to me since my uncle's MTB sank in that storm was connected. But unless I could join all the dots up, my life really was going to completely spiral out of control.

* * *

My boss made no attempt to directly meet La Princesa, the woman now in charge of the Chilean cartel, for a long time. I presumed he'd decided it was better to keep some distance between us. In any case, the original deal had been rubber-stamped by those two Chileans who'd turned up on Ibiza, so there was no real reason for us to meet her in person. All arrangements were carried out on cell phones and through intermediaries. What we didn't know wouldn't hurt us, and the less we knew about La Princesa and her associates the better it would be for us.

There was another reason why we avoided meeting her. There had been constant rumours that La Princesa wouldn't last long, ever since she took over the cartel following her father's murder. But after nearly a year at the helm, it had become clear that nothing could be further from the truth.

CHAPTER FIFTEEN
BUSINESS AND PLEASURE

Having studiously avoided meeting La Princesa for almost a year, the cartel's representative in Madrid informed us that she wanted to discuss some "new arrangements". This included plans to step up production of cocaine back in Chile, so that the size of each load could be increased.

The night before we were due to fly out to Madrid, my boss rang and cried off with "the flu" and sent me on my own. I sensed he was having marriage problems at the time, so I didn't question his decision. But I was more thrown by something else he said on the phone: *"Be careful. I heard she's fucked up beyond repair."* It seemed a strange thing to say, especially after that earlier breakdown in trust between us. Now he was going out of his way to warn me about something, so maybe I shouldn't have been so black and white about our relationship. His advice left me feeling oddly *more* secure because it seemed to imply the Brit still trusted me, even if I wasn't sure if I felt the same way about him.

The hotel chosen by the cartel turned out to be one of Madrid's most expensive, which meant I looked a little out of place with my ponytail and jeans. I was met by two henchmen in the lobby area, who took me up to La Princesa's suite. In the elevator, I explained that my own boss was sick and couldn't make it, and they looked a little worried and insisted I tell their boss as soon as I met her. By the time we reached the hotel suite, I'd become a little nervous about what to expect.

La Princesa turned out to be a tall, statuesque blonde who looked more like the CEO of a FTSE 100 company than the leader of a drug cartel. Her nails were immaculately manicured, varnished in blood red, and she wore a neatly fitting designer trouser suit.

She asked why my boss wasn't there and also inferred that she'd met him before. I was thrown because I'd thought they didn't know each other. When I asked her if she wanted to postpone the meeting until my boss could be there, she backtracked and insisted we go ahead.

Then her eyes narrowed.

"I'm sure we've met before. You look very familiar."

"I don't think so," I replied. "I would have remembered."

This was followed by an awkward silence.

"So here we are," she eventually said.

I nodded, unsure how to respond.

"Who do *you* think killed my father?" she asked, without a hint of emotion in her voice.

"I thought your people took care of that when they came to Ibiza?" I replied.

"That's true, but someone must have told the chief about my father's movements before he spoke to the police in Santiago," La Princesa said, leaving her words hanging in the air, while studying me closely. "I just wondered what you thought about that?" she added.

She immediately followed this up with some inane questions that ranged from the weather in Madrid to the quality of the wine from Chile, before saying: "Thank you for coming to see me. It's been very enlightening."

That was it? Game over? It felt as if I'd flown all the way to Madrid just so La Princesa could ask me to my face if I knew anything about the murder of her father. Was she trying to tell me something, or had someone told her I was involved?

As I got up to leave, she asked me to have dinner with her, almost as an afterthought. I hadn't been expecting it. When I hesitated, she started backtracking.

"You're probably tired after the journey, so…

"I'd love to."

I don't know to this day why I said it, but I did.

It would turn out to be one of the biggest mistakes of my life.

* * *

I felt oddly nervous that evening as I sat at a table in the hotel restaurant waiting for La Princesa to join me. She'd made me feel quite uncomfortable at the earlier meeting, yet I was intrigued by her.

She turned up 10 minutes late and insisted I sat next to her in a booth, rather than opposite her. I presumed she didn't want anyone overhearing our conversation. Within a couple of minutes, she began brushing my knee to emphasize points, even when it was something as unimportant as what starter to choose. I let her hold court and she was so expansive about everything that I started to suspect she'd taken a line of cocaine. Soon the wine was flowing, and instead of her hand brushing my knee she started leaving it there.

As the alcohol kicked in, I found myself actually enjoying La Princesa's company, despite the icy ruthlessness I saw in her eyes whenever I looked into them. We discussed a wide range of topics but never delved into anything particularly personal. No big surprise there.

After we'd each drunk a cognac at the end of the meal, she insisted on paying the bill on condition I went to her room for a nightcap. I knew it was madness but, as usual, I just went with the flow. We never got round to drinking a nightcap because within seconds of walking into her room, we were pulling each other's clothes off. It was frenzied and there was an undercurrent of desperation because we didn't pause for breath.

After it was over, she offered me a puff on her cigarette as we lay next to each other on the bed, and we both agreed that it had been just what we needed. It was such a strangely clinical thing to say to each other after making love. It reduced everything to a question of need rather than passion, which made it nothing more than a one-night stand for both of us.

I was about to leave her hotel room when she asked me to stay and chat with her. She sounded softer and less assured than at any time during the entire evening.

"I never wanted to be in this business," she said. "My father sent me to Madrid to study. I fell in love with this city and didn't want to go back to Chile."

She admitted knowing her father's mistress La Patrona and how she'd often stayed at her apartment in Madrid.

"She was a good person. We were like sisters in many ways," she explained. "She understood who I was."

I was so surprised by her mentioning La Patrona that I didn't know what to say. But as it sank it, I started to feel some kind of connection with her. She must have sensed that, because then she asked me if I knew La Patrona had been her father's mistress in Madrid. When I nodded, she looked oddly at me for a few moments until I explained that the Chileans who'd flown into Ibiza after her father's murder had told me.

I asked her what her father had felt about her being close to La Patrona. That seemed to throw her because she thought very carefully about her reply before saying: "He was happy that I'd accepted her as his lover, but when we got friendlier, I think he became a bit jealous. Typical man, eh?"

I remember thinking at the time that she didn't sound particularly heartbroken that her father was dead. I was lost in my thoughts when her eyes narrowed and she repeated what she'd said earlier about being convinced we'd met before. This time, she asked me the specific date I'd been in Madrid meeting La Patrona. I hesitated while trying to work it out and noticed her nodding slightly to herself.

It suddenly clicked that I'd seen her on the morning I left La Patrona's apartment in Madrid. She'd been the young brunette woman who'd walked out of the lift and let herself into the apartment with a key. She couldn't have realized who I was back then, unless La Patrona told her, and I was fairly certain she wouldn't have done that.

I was obliged to tell her the date I'd met La Patrona in Madrid, even though it would help her work out we were lovers. But after I told her the date, she just nodded her head, thanked me and carried on telling me more about her friendship with La Patrona. She told me how the child that La Patrona had with her father had died soon after her murder, due to complications linked to the child's disability.

I felt so uncomfortable by this time that I made out I had to meet a local criminal and needed to leave immediately. As I got dressed, she looked up at me from the bed. She was laying completely naked with her chin resting on one hand, tilting her head slightly to one side.

"Am I as good as her in bed?"

"Sorry?"

"Am I as good as her in bed?"

"Who?"

"The love of your life, of course."

"There's never been one," I answered quickly.

She laughed, sat on the edge of the bed and looked up at me.

"Oh, everyone has one of those," she said, pausing. "Even your boss's wife."

I tried to ignore her and continued getting dressed.

"Hasn't he told you?" she continued. "She's having a fling with that cute Cuban guy. He's offered to buy our cocaine at a higher price than you're paying."

She tilted her head again as her words sank in.

"He's obsessed with fucking over your boss," she added in a naughty, almost childish voice. "I guess that's all about his wife."

She stood up naked at the end of the bed, beckoned me over and offered her cheek for me to kiss goodbye. I could feel her breath on my ear as she whispered: "Prices are doubling from next week. I hope your boss can afford it."

* * *

My legs were shaking as I stood in the elevator going down to the lobby. If I'm to be 100 per cent honest, a horrible sense of doom and gloom was gradually coming over me. Yet that in itself was bizarrely tempered with the after-thrill that comes from an exciting, spontaneous sexual encounter. And this diverse series of emotions perfectly summed up what my relationship with La Princesa already felt like.

If I'd paused for a moment and thought it all through, I'd have realized how insane it was to mix business and pleasure.

CHAPTER SIXTEEN
TAKE-DOWN

The following morning, I phoned the Brit from Madrid airport before getting the flight back to Ibiza and told him about the price hike.

"She can go fuck herself if she thinks she can just rip us off," he said.

I didn't bother asking him if he'd met her before. My boss's anger on the phone took me aback because I'd never known him like this before. On the plane back to Ibiza my meltdown about sleeping with La Princesa worsened. I felt as if I'd betrayed my boss and the rest of the gang by stepping across the line.

After disembarking from the plane, I ended up wandering through Ibiza airport's arrivals area in a complete daze, lost in my thoughts until I reached the main exit to the terminal building where I planned to hail a taxi. I didn't notice my boss's classic black Seat roll up alongside me until the rear passenger window wound down and he ordered me to get in. He was the last person I wanted to see at that moment, but I put on a happy face and jumped in beside him.

Before we'd even left the airport perimeter, he'd repeated his earlier pledge that he wasn't going to be ripped off by the

Chileans' proposed price increase. But at least his aggressive reaction to that helped me avoid any uncomfortable questions about La Princesa. And despite still feeling like I'd betrayed the Brit, I also avoided mentioning what La Princesa had said about the Cuban's affair with his wife. He ordered me to call La Princesa and tell her we were "adjusting our finances" in order to come back to her with a higher offer for her cocaine. He explained it was a stalling move, which would hopefully give us time to find a new supplier.

After he'd dropped me at my mother's villa, I called La Princesa to tell her this, and she informed me we could have no more than one week, before switching the conversation to how nice it had been to meet me and how she hoped we could enjoy some more time together soon. I was completely thrown because I'd thought we'd only had a one-night stand. Maybe she was just being polite. But her playful tone made it sound a lot more than that. Then I thought, why the fuck should it matter anyway?

When I phoned the Brit and told him about La Princesa's deadline, he got even more antsy and insisted I go straight to his office at the warehouse so we could further discuss the deal. I was unhappy about the state he seemed to be in, so decided it would be the perfect opportunity to straighten out a few impending matters. The moment I walked into his office and saw the tense expression on his face, I knew I had no choice but to confront him.

"What's going on?" I said. "You seem so pissed off the whole time. Have I done something wrong?"

"It's not you," he said, almost apologetically.

He paused for a few moments as he stood by his office window looking down into the main part of his warehouse, which was crammed with furniture.

"You know I always kept all this shit away from my kids," the Brit said. "I didn't want my wife or them to ever be in the firing line. Not knowing what I did for a job gave them protection, in a sense."

But, he explained that in recent months, his wife had started confronting him about being a criminal. At first, he denied it and they started arguing a lot. Then she asked him if he had had anything to do with the death of the old Guardia Civil chief.

"That was the final straw," explained the Brit. "Somebody must have been telling her stuff, so I confronted her about it and she confessed she was having an affair with the Cuban. He's had her spying on me since the first time he knocked her off more than six months ago. No wonder he's been one step ahead of us a lot of the time recently. She probably doesn't even realize how much she's helped him," he said. "She's a fucking security risk to all of us."

He said he'd even considered hiring a hitman to kill the Cuban but had decided not to when his wife warned him she'd commit suicide if anything happened to her lover.

"I couldn't do that to my kids," said the Brit.

So he'd decided to destroy the Cuban's drug business instead. His wife's affair had been the main reason the Brit had taken the plunge into the cocaine business in the first place. He wanted to stop the Cuban at all costs.

I tried not to look surprised but inside I was reeling. I'd always respected the Brit for being so focused, but I had to admit it now seemed as if he'd taken his eye right off the ball, which is never a good thing to do in this game. It was also obvious that my boss and the Cuban were being played by La Princesa. Maybe that was the reason why she had slept with me.

It was in her interests to have us all at each other's throats, so she could hike the price of her product up even higher. What we did to each other on the ground was of no concern to her. I didn't point any of this out to my boss, though.

We agreed that, in a perfect world, we'd have stepped back for a while and negotiated La Princesa down on the price of her cocaine. But the Cuban wasn't going to go away.

"She told you about my wife's affair, didn't she?" the Brit suddenly asked me during that meeting in the warehouse office.

I said nothing at first because I didn't want to humiliate him any further because then he might end up doing something really stupid, something that could spark a full-scale drugs war.

"I didn't tell you I met her once, before you went to Madrid," he said. "I thought it was for a serious meeting but afterwards she made it clear she wanted me to go to bed with her. I told her I loved my wife and turned her down, she got really mad and that's why I told you to be careful."

After my boss finished talking, I noticed him looking straight at me in a similar way to how he had done in the days and weeks after my uncle's boat sank.

"I hope that bitch hasn't fucked with your head," he added.

I had little doubt he was thinking that I might no longer be on his side because I most likely had slept with La Princesa. But he'd never told me about how he'd met La Princesa before I went to that first meeting with her in Madrid, which meant he was hiding stuff from me as well.

Maybe that was the moment I should have told him what happened with La Princesa? But once I'd done that, there would have been no going back on it. In any case, he'd end up even more convinced I was trying to screw him over if I told him. That's the trouble with the underworld. You can't be 100 per cent honest, even when you want to be.

We only had ourselves to blame for a lot of what was happening, though. We'd spent so many years in a safe little bubble in Ibiza that we thought we were virtually untouchable. We'd taken so much stuff for granted because we believed we'd always control the island's drug supply.

Professional crime thrives on death and destruction. I'd considered myself to be above the usual riff-raff, but really I was no better than any of them. So I went back to Plan A and pressed my boss to agree to pay La Princesa whatever she wanted for her cocaine.

After I'd said it, he sat looking down at his feet for ages before lifting his head and staring straight at me, taking a long, deep breath and saying: "The bitch can fuck off. I'll find another supplier. No one holds me to ransom." Still looking at me, he added: "And if the Cuban buys her shit then he'll have a war on his hands."

The hatred my boss felt towards the Cuban and La Princesa had weakened his ability to make clear, precise decisions. In this game, when things get personal it usually only ends one way.

A war was the last thing we needed, especially with my boss falling apart. And my non-violence code of practice was about to completely go up in smoke.

* * *

A few hours later, after running a few errands, I arrived at my mother's villa to find her in tears and extremely drunk. My boss had been there with three gang members and they'd turned the attic upside down looking for something. She slurred that none of them would tell her what they wanted.

My mother pleaded with me not to confront him because she was scared of what might happen. I ignored her and marched out of the house, but she stumbled after me and stood in front of my car begging me not to leave her on her own. So instead, I went back into the house and called my boss. He sounded drunk and slammed the phone down the moment he heard my voice. He didn't pick up any of my subsequent calls.

I had little doubt he was being hit hard by his wife's affair, but that still didn't give him the right to upset my mother. In the back of my mind, I knew I couldn't turn up in a fury at his house, partly because I didn't want to drag my boss's family into it all but also because his wife would most likely tell the Cuban everything. So I took a few deep breaths and decided to just concentrate on looking after my mother that evening.

All night, I couldn't stop wondering what he'd been looking for in my mother's attic. Maybe he'd planned to steal all the spare cash he knew I kept in a stash somewhere on the property. But why would he bother doing that?

The next morning, I drove round to his house and his wife told me he'd already left for the airport. When she asked me what was wrong and where he'd gone, I shrugged my shoulders and said I didn't know.

* * *

Iberia's early morning Boeing 727 flight to Madrid was heading down the runway for takeoff as I swung into the airport car park less than half an hour after leaving my boss's house. I found out from a desk clerk I knew that he was due to catch a connecting flight from the Spanish capital to Cali, Colombia, later that morning.

The rest of that summer's day in 2001 felt really weird. I left the airport and headed into the Old Town in the direction of the furniture warehouse until I remembered there was no point because my boss wasn't here.

In many ways, I am a creature of habit. Despite my upbringing amid so much chaos, I like to have a routine and my life in the Brit's gang had given me that structure in my life. Now there was a vacuum, and I was having to think about life beyond the gang. I didn't know what was going to happen when he came back to Ibiza, but I'd have to confront him about his "raid" on my mother's villa.

Yet in the recent past, he'd proved much more honourable than me in many other ways. He'd resisted the temptation to sleep with La Princesa, and a lot of what she'd done recently may well have been down to the humiliation she'd felt at being rejected by him. Had I walked right into a trap? Or maybe my boss had lied to me, and they had slept together and then he'd dumped her.

I ended up back home around mid-afternoon. My mother was having a siesta, which often meant she wouldn't emerge again from her bedroom until the following morning. So I watched a bit of mindless television before retiring very early to bed to read a book. But I couldn't concentrate on reading because my mind kept wandering back to what I'd discovered over the previous 24 hours.

I finally got to sleep at about 2 a.m. but was woken up less than two hours later by a phone call. I presumed it would be the Brit finally coming to his senses after arriving in Colombia. But it was La Princesa.

"I'm so sorry to hear about what has happened," she said.

Her voice was flat and distant. I didn't know what she was talking about.

"One of my friends in Colombia just called me with the news."

"What news?" I said.

She said my boss had been travelling in a convoy of cartel vehicles north of Cali airport when they were stopped by an army unit manning an isolated roadblock. The soldiers turned out to be narcos wearing stolen uniforms, and they shot the Brit and three other men in the convoy. They deliberately left their bodies on the roadside.

"The cartel thought your boss was an undercover DEA informant," she said. "Those Colombians are so fucking paranoid."

Then – almost as an afterthought – she added: "So you're running things now, right?"

I was in such a state of shock, I didn't know what to say.

She exploited the awkward silence by adding: "I think we'll work well together, so I'm going to put the price back to what it was."

"Okay," I answered hesitantly, saying the first thing that came into my head.

"Don't feel bad about what's happened to him, either," she added.

"What d'you mean?" I asked.

"None of this is your fault," she said, with an intonation I didn't understand. I hung up the phone.

My gut reaction the moment I heard about the killing was to walk away from everything. It felt like fucking bad karma, putting it mildly. But I hesitated. There were some complex, unanswered questions when it came to my boss's murder. Did the Cuban tip the Colombian cartel off or, more likely, was it La Princesa, angry that my boss had decided to find a new supplier? Before I went anywhere, I needed to find out.

CHAPTER SEVENTEEN
DAMAGED

In September 2001, the 9/11 attacks occurred in the US and the world was turned upside down. Transportation routes for cocaine from Latin America via Mexico came under incredibly close scrutiny from US law enforcement. There were even allegations that narco money-launderers had helped clean cash used by the hijackers themselves. It seemed to many in the underworld that the DEA and other US agencies were using the terror attacks to try and crack down on crime across the globe, even if it had no direct connections to terror.

Transportation of cocaine from the cartel in Chile and our cannabis supply route from Morocco were both suspended until brand new operations could be worked out that law enforcement would know nothing about. I was relieved because it meant I could delay announcing I was quitting and avoid upsetting La Princesa for the moment.

Ibiza itself had for some time been far too busy when it came to the drugs scene, and this had attracted a lot of unwanted attention over the previous few years, so I increasingly began to think it was the perfect time for me to walk away from it all. For the moment, I agreed with La Princesa that we suspend all shipments for one month, by which time the situation should have become clearer, hopefully. But it was obvious from her tone that she was more worried about her loss of income than the likelihood that we'd all end up in prison or dead if we pushed our luck. It was a big moment in history, and I'd tried to convince her we needed to treat it with caution.

I desperately needed this long overdue breathing space. I was still in complete shock about my boss's murder, which made me feel doubly guilty about sleeping with La Princesa, knowing that my own boss had turned her down. I knew he had been in the middle of a meltdown because of his marriage problems, but I never expected it to lead to his killing. Despite our differences towards the end of his life, he'd been a father figure to me in many ways.

His death made me question the entire drugs business. How had I allowed myself to become so immersed in something doomed to one day explode into tiny pieces? I needed to wake up and deal with what had happened and act on my good instincts as opposed to my bad habits.

* * *

Almost exactly four weeks later, a text turned up from La Princesa. It excitedly explained that Mexico's narco gangsters were already back in business, having opened brand new transport hubs from where her South American cocaine could be shipped to the rest of the world. She also said in the text that she'd booked what she described as "our favourite hotel" in Madrid and we were to meet there the following day.

I immediately tried to call her back to cancel her visit. I wanted to tell her I was quitting the drugs business, but she wasn't picking up. Then I figured it was probably best to tell her everything in person anyway. I had no idea what to really expect from such a meeting. I appreciated I might have to play her along first and then tell her the truth about my plans.

She was already waiting in the restaurant of the hotel when I arrived from Madrid airport. The moment I sat down she started talking nonstop and kept brushing my arm every time she wanted to make a point. It was very similar to the first time we'd had dinner, except this time I was much more anxious because I wanted to get in and out of there as quickly and painlessly as possible.

When she began dashing to the toilet at 10-minute intervals, I knew she was snorting cocaine again. She also hardly touched her food, insisting that she was on a diet and excitedly telling me how much money we could make together. I sat back and let her take over for a while. It was a stupid move, but I thought I needed time to work out the best way to handle the situation. The trouble is that by letting her run the meeting, I'd enabled her to make it even harder for me to tell her I was quitting.

She said she had plans to organize her own transport facilities directly from South America, which would eventually cut out the Mexicans as well as the fishermen of the Atlantic coastline of Galicia, north-west Spain. This would give her cartel bigger profit margins in the long run. With Europe now on the verge of taking over as the largest cocaine market on the globe, it certainly made complete, economic sense.

She pointed out that since 9/11, the global narcotics marketplace had begun undergoing enormous changes. Brand new markets would soon emerge, including the eastern European nations as well as the newly viable state of Russia, where cocaine was expected to take off now that its citizens were no longer ruled by the communists and had money in their pockets.

After we'd finished the meal, I insisted on paying for it, and while I was waiting for the bill, I started trying to work the conversation round to my decision to quit.

"So what happened between you and my boss before I met you?" I asked her.

"I was wondering when you'd ask me about that," she said. "Do you really want to know?"

"Yes."

In retrospect, it was a clumsy way to try and regain control of the situation because then the absolute opposite occurred.

"Let's not talk about it here," she suddenly said.

So I had no choice but to accept her invitation to visit her suite for "a nightcap". I still hadn't told her I was planning to quit. Worse still, I realized as we entered the suite, it was the same one where we'd slept together previously, except it was filled with flowers this time. The size and intention of the gesture was beyond what I was feeling, and I should have walked out of that hotel room there and then, but I felt compelled to stay because I wanted to know what had happened between her and my boss, as well as finally telling her I was quitting.

She knew I was nervous and tried to put me at my ease by asking what I thought of the flowers in the suite. It just made things worse, because the nicer she tried to be, the more awkward it felt.

I kept thinking about my boss and wondering if she'd played a role in his murder because he'd done what I hadn't and rejected her. Was everything that had just happened a direct result of this one event? There was I thinking I was tough enough to handle all these types of heavy situations, but in reality this was all completely beyond my usual remit in life.

When I finally got up the courage to bring the conversation back to her and my boss, she laughed it off.

"It was no big deal," she said. "He came here, we did some business and he went home to his wife and kids."

Before I could ask her anything more, she kissed me. I don't know why to this day, but I didn't push her away.

An hour later, after we'd made love, I recovered my composure and decided to explain to her that her friend the Cuban had found a Colombian cartel to supply him with cocaine and was trying to take over Ibiza's drugs underworld. It was getting too dangerous, I told her, and I felt it was time to get out.

"You're quitting?" she asked.

I nodded.

"Are you fucking serious?" she said.

I shrugged my shoulders and tried to look apologetic.

"You cannot do this," she said through gritted teeth, under her breath.

"I have to," I replied.

"But I thought we were doing this together?" she said, her voice quivering with emotion.

Then she suddenly began crying. I tried to console her, but it was difficult to be genuinely warm and empathetic as there was some part of me wondering if these were fake, manipulative tears. I simply didn't trust her.

Yet I deserved all this, in many ways. I'd been no more honest than her, really. Maybe we were two like-minded people after all who were fated to be together? So I held her close as she cried into my shoulder and tried to play for time while I contemplated my next move. Everything was fucking with my head, and I needed it to be clear at all times.

After she'd calmed down, we lay there looking up at the mirrored ceiling, holding hands, and didn't say another word to each other for ages. I watched her eyes in the reflection as she stared at herself lying there. Unsettlingly, there was a slight smile on her face. I wondered whether she felt something for me or if it simply meant she thought she still had me in her pocket.

Eventually she lit up a cigarette, offering me a puff on it and and said: "Tell me something about you," she paused. "Please."

I didn't know how to answer her, so I tried to smile back.

I felt uncomfortable because it was the first time she'd asked me anything personal. I eventually told her how I'd been my mother's carer for years. I also mentioned some of her wartime experiences before I was born. It was a relief not to talk about drugs and money for a change. She seemed to be listening very carefully to me as I explained everything, and that did make me feel closer to her.

When I'd finished, she said: "Your mother and my father sound quite alike. Isn't it strange how we both learned to survive on our own from an early age without knowing who our parents really were? And in the end, it's their secrets that taint your entire life."

Then she hesitated, so I smiled reassuringly up at the mirror above us.

"Do you think everything bad from the past catches up with you in the end?" she asked.

"Probably," I answered. "Why?"

"It's not important," she said.

"Then why did you say it?"

"I'm not sure," she replied.

"Come on," I said. "Tell me."

She sighed and then began explaining to me how her father had sexually abused her for much of her childhood. Her voice remained calm and controlled as she spoke, but that did nothing to hide the damage.

"I thought what he was doing to me was normal, even though it felt wrong," she explained. "He only stopped because I reached puberty. I thought he was rejecting me because I hadn't been loving enough towards him."

She said it took years before she even admitted to herself what had happened.

"That's when it finally hit home. I couldn't sleep or eat. I felt suicidal and I thought it was all my fault."

La Princesa said she even started taking cocaine to kill the pain and in defiance of her father, as he always told her never to take it.

"When he did find out I was on it, I was more scared of him than I had been when he was abusing me," she said. "What happened undoubtedly impacted on my ability to maintain a healthy perspective of life. For years, I'd thought what he was doing to me was 'normal' because I had no one to tell about it. My mother would never have believed me. In any case, she was even more terrified of my father than I was."

As she spoke, the ruthless, cold-blooded drug cartel boss seemed to have morphed into an extremely vulnerable and sensitive person. So instead of reiterating to her that I was quitting the narcotics trade, I found myself wanting to 'fix' her and help make her feel happier. I hugged her tight and we rocked back and forth in silence for a few minutes. Beneath that tough exterior was someone with a damaged core of goodness.

Looking back, I was naïve. If I'd taken a proper step back, I would have realized I was falling for a woman who'd clearly inherited a lot of her father's most chilling habits, despite the fact he'd abused her. That should have been a warning sign in itself. Instead, I did nothing but encourage her. In the end, we sat there rocking back and forth until she seemed to fall asleep in my arms.

I woke up a few hours later to find her silhouette sitting cross-legged on the end of the bed watching me. She was back-lit by the soft pre-dawn light pouring into the hotel room. I couldn't be certain, but it looked as if she'd been awake most of the night. The rest of that day in Madrid was spent visiting shops and restaurants, holding hands everywhere, and we didn't once mention business. I bought her a bracelet and she insisted I accepted a chunky gold signate ring from her. After she slid it onto my finger, she said: "Now you're mine."

That evening we ended up in the shady corner of a bar around the corner from the hotel. I went up to ask the barmaid for two glasses of wine. By the time I got back to the table, she had a thunderous expression on her face.

When I asked her what was wrong, she snapped back at me: "She's pretty isn't she?"

"Who?" I asked, knowing full well she meant the barmaid.

"Don't ever cheat on me," she said, getting up from the table. "Because I'll know if you have."

She walked out of the bar and left without saying another word.

I paid the bill and caught up with her outside, but she ignored me and carried on walking towards the hotel.

That's when I thought back to what my old boss had said to me after he cried off accompanying me to that first meeting with her in Madrid. *"Be careful. I heard she's fucked up beyond repair."* He already knew from his encounter with her what she was like, but I'd ignored his warning. I still found her intriguing, despite her anger in the bar and everything else. Yet in the back of my mind, I also kept turning over her obvious disappointment when my boss didn't turn up in Madrid for that first meeting.

I still hadn't properly got to the bottom of what had really happened. There were still so many unanswered questions that controlled my life.

* * *

I slept on the sofa in our hotel suite lined with flowers that night because she was still angry with me after that incident in the bar. It was extremely uncomfortable, so I kept waking up, not helped by a disturbing series of dreams that all centred around her. In one, she seemed to be about to kill me. In another she was on the verge of jumping out a window. Each one was so vivid that, when I woke up, it took me quite a few seconds to realize where I was.

So when she really did wake me up in the early hours to apologize, I was genuinely thrown. She then wanted to have sex. I didn't object. That was a big mistake because it immediately felt mechanical and mindless. Even her voice sounded different. It was as if she'd turned into another person. When I tried to get off her and go back to the sofa, she took that as a rejection, grabbed me angrily and looked maniacally into my eyes.

"I love you," she said.

I didn't respond.

"Let's make as much money as we can and then run off together to a desert island."

When I still didn't answer, she got out of bed and went to the bathroom, slamming the door behind her. I tried to join her, but she pushed me out as if we were complete strangers and I'd just invaded her space. Then she got dressed and left the room, without saying goodbye. I was relieved in a sense, although I knew that wouldn't be the end of it.

CHAPTER EIGHTEEN
THE AFRICAN GENTLEMEN

Later that morning, I flew from Madrid to London for my father's wedding to his long-term German girlfriend. After checking into a hotel in Piccadilly, in the centre of London, I walked across Hyde Park to where I was meeting him for lunch and a catch-up about his impending marriage. I also wanted to discuss my property empire, which he remained in charge of.

As I walked past Buckingham Palace, I noticed a man about 30 yards behind me. He looked like the same person I'd passed in Piccadilly when I'd left the hotel 10 minutes earlier. I couldn't be sure if he was following me but made a note to check again later.

A few minutes after this strange moment, I walked into the wine bar. I knew my father had problems from the moment I saw the expression on his face. He seemed especially nervous when we began discussing all the property investments he'd been handling for me. He eventually admitted he'd been dipping into my cash reserves to pay off his latest gambling debts. He'd even been taking out mortgages against the value of those properties bought with the proceeds of the drugs I'd handled.

I wanted to be angry with him but it just wasn't in my nature to be like that, or at least I didn't want it to be. I told him I'd find the money to pay off the mortgages and tried to cheer him up, as he was getting married the following day after all. I realized, yet again, I'd morphed into being the parent to my parents. The older they got, the more I seemed to have to look after them.

As I walked back across Hyde Park afterwards, I noticed the same man from earlier following me from a distance all the way back to the hotel. If he was a tail, he wasn't a very good one. I was tempted to confront him, but I knew from working with these people that he'd just deny everything, so I let it go and tried to enjoy the rest of my day.

* * *

That evening, I met up with my oldest and best friend from school for dinner. He was the only "outsider" I'd ever told about my career in drugs. After trying to persuade me to quit many years earlier, he'd eventually agreed to use his legal skills to handle all the conveyancing on the properties my father had been purchasing in London with my illicit cash.

He knew all about my father's gambling and how it was impacting on my finances, which was one of the other reasons I had to meet him. At first, I was irritated that he hadn't told me before. However, it soon became clear that he'd been very worried that my father was in deep trouble but hadn't wanted to "inform" on him. He rightly said it was up to my father to tell me what had happened, not him.

We ended up consoling each other about our respective fathers, who were far from normal when it came to parenting. Despite having ruled as president of the DRWA for many years, my friend's father had now been labelled a despot following accusations of election fraud and human rights abuses by his soldiers. My friend had just started explaining how disgusted he was about it when I noticed his eyes darting to two African men in suits sitting on the other side of the restaurant. They were definitely watching us. When I asked him who they were, he said that they worked for his father, who'd ordered them to keep an eye on him, and that this had pissed him off big time. He insisted we pay the bill and leave the restaurant because of them.

My friend had got into a cab outside and I was waiting for another one when the same two men politely introduced themselves to me as being from the DRWA's London embassy. I was intrigued. Even though I knew my friend had been upset by their presence, I wanted to know why they'd come to talk to me if they were following him on behalf of his father, so I accepted their invitation to have a drink at a nearby bar. The moment we sat down, they mentioned 9/11 and how it must have seriously impacted on "business opportunities" for people like myself.

I said nothing but realized that if they'd been monitoring my friend in London then they must have found out about my property portfolio. I now couldn't leave until I'd discovered what else they knew. They went on to disclose how my best friend's father, their president, had also been acquiring property in London, ever since he'd become leader. I was sure his son didn't know the full extent of this property empire, as they hadn't spoken in a long time.

Their voices lowered as they began to explain to me that the president was looking for new multi-national business opportunities to improve the economy of his country. They said the type of business didn't really matter because the president's priority was to save his country. Enthusiastically trying to sell me the geography of the place, they said it would make the perfect hub to handle and transport narcotics, as there were hundreds of miles of deserted coastline, unpopulated mangrove swamps just inland and deserted roads to transport drugs north to Europe and beyond.

The president wanted to turn his tiny, war-ravaged, poverty-stricken country into a narco-state. It had been done elsewhere in the world, so why not in his little nation? I could see some definite parallels with Ibiza, which had evolved into a narco-state of sorts because it was in the middle of Europe and drugs had greatly helped its economy after centuries of being a neglected and sparsely populated island.

The president's men also explained that their leader was offering a money-laundering facility through the country's banking system. In exchange, the president wanted a percentage of all the cash earned from the drugs coming through DRWA. The two embassy gentlemen insisted most of that would be put back into the tiny nation's infrastructure to improve roads, schools and all the other important services that had been neglected for decades.

I stopped the two men there and asked them to thank their president for his kind and generous offer but said I was no longer in the drugs business, so I couldn't help them. They seemed surprised by my announcement but said very little more. Just before they got up to leave, one of them handed me his card and said he hoped I'd change my mind and call him. Both men then shook my hand politely and left the bar.

I walked back across the West End to my hotel, relieved that I'd said no and hopeful that this would mark the start of a new life away from crime. I was glad I'd told La Princesa earlier that I was finally quitting and at least now I could do it with a clear conscience.

This time I really had to remain strong and steadfastly determined not to be lured back into criminality.

* * *

My father's wedding turned out to be a quiet affair attended by a couple of their friends, and I was the main witnesses at a registry office in Paddington. My father should have looked happy, but he seemed extremely agitated throughout the ceremony. I pulled him aside at the reception in a local pub and told him not to worry about all his debts. It was their special day and I wanted them to enjoy the moment. But my reassuring words did nothing to help. He ended up having a drunken row with his bride just before I left the pub. I interceded and took my father outside to once again try to calm him down.

Outside, in a low tone, he confessed that he'd not been taking out legal mortgages, as he'd earlier claimed. Instead, he'd been borrowing money from my best friend's father, the president, and he owed more than 2 million pounds. He said that that very morning just before his wedding, what sounded like the same two gentlemen from the DRWA embassy that I'd met the previous evening had threatened to kill him if he didn't pay the money back within a month or persuade me to find a cartel to set up their drugs operation in the DRWA. My stomach sank.

Everything happening seemed to be my fault. If I hadn't started working in the drug business, I wouldn't have got in the habit of paying off my father's gambling debts and employing him in my property business. The men from the DRWA wouldn't be trying to persuade me to trade drugs through their nation and my father would have simply fallen into debt rather than fearing for his life.

When I told my father I'd work out a solution, he said to forget what he'd said, as I was almost out now and it would be madness to go back into the drug business because of his irresponsibility. I told him that we should sleep on it, even though I doubted we'd even have that long to make a decision, or many options to choose from.

After I got back to my hotel that night, I got a call from one of the president's men. He asked me if I'd changed my mind. I took a deep breath and told him that, of course, I had. I knew I'd regret it, but sometimes in life you have to weigh up stuff and be pragmatic and realistic about your options. I didn't want any harm to come to my father. And if I'm to be entirely honest about it, I felt a twinge of excitement thinking about the challenges that lay ahead. The embassy man sounded pleased at my decision and said that, as a thank you, the president would wipe out all the debts my father had incurred once the cartel was up and running in the DRWA.

It's a confusing feeling to know you've just taken a monumental step backwards into the heart of darkness – a combination of extreme trepidation and exhilaration as the adrenaline kicks in. I should have thought it through more carefully. I'd completely failed to learn from my previous mistakes, and now I was back on the edge of a precipice. But it was all down to me.

Over the following 24 hours, I researched everything there was to know about the Democratic Republic of West Africa.

I needed to know what I was getting myself into. I spent six hours studying archive material in the British Library. I'd also convinced myself that if – as they'd promised – the president's "tax" would help provide DRWA citizens with good schools, public transport and roads, then maybe there was good side to all this.

The most disturbing aspect of it all was that after making my decision to stay in the drugs game, I felt an even bigger buzz of excitement than that day I'd sailed out of the bay from the secret beach on my uncle's MTB. Maybe I'd finally morphed into a full-on criminal after all and needed to come to terms with that.

I called La Princesa and asked her to meet me in London. She sounded delighted to hear from me and rightly presumed I must have changed my mind or else I wouldn't have phoned her.

I was walking slowly across a minefield and the chances of being destroyed were increasing with every footstep. Now there really was no turning back.

CHAPTER NINETEEN
OLD HABITS

At 5.30 a.m. the next morning, I was awoken by a loud bang on the door of my London hotel room. For a few moments, I didn't move. Then there was an even louder knock. I feared it might be connected to that man who'd been following me in London. Whoever it was, they knew I was in there, so there was no point in ignoring it.

When I opened the door, I found La Princesa standing there clutching a bottle of champagne in her hand, smiling.

"Happy Birthday," she said.

Without another word, she pushed me four or five steps back into the room and onto the bed.

After our love-making, it dawned on me that perhaps our relationship, if you can call it that, was fuelled by loneliness. We both had no one else in the world to turn to. The sex was comforting and reassuring rather than thrilling, although we'd not admitted this to each other since the first time we'd slept together.

"How did you know it was my birthday?" I asked her, as we lay on the bed together.

"I have my spies," she said playfully. "More importantly, why have you decided to work with me after all?"

It was a fair enough question, since I'd done a complete about-turn and, in the underworld, criminals pick up on that sort of stuff.

"There's a lot of reasons," I said.

"Like what?" she asked.

Her light interrogation immediately made me feel uncomfortable, but I knew I had to answer her properly or else she'd think I was doing something against her. I began by telling her about the threats against my father. But she wasn't very empathetic about his gambling addiction, so I put my reasons into a business format she'd more clearly understand. I explained that our relaunch as a cartel following 9/11 would require a huge reboot anyway. We needed tighter security for the entire operation and that would mean much more money. This, I explained, was where the DRWA came in.

She looked perplexed at first, which wasn't helped by the fact she didn't know where the DRWA was. So I explained the geography of the place and how it was a perfect transit point for her produce. She didn't even realize that planes could be flown across the Atlantic directly to the DRWA. I revealed how the president had offered to give us the freedom of his tiny nation, which would enable us to transport, package and distribute our drugs through the DRWA. It would be much safer than in Europe, which had become increasingly over-policed since 9/11.

But all she said after I'd explained everything was, "Okay." Despite my reassurances, she still sounded uncertain. So I suggested she supply cannabis to the European market by growing it in Chile and flying it over in the same aircraft that brought the cocaine shipments. That brought the breakthrough I'd hoped for, because anything that would help her make more money was too tempting for her to turn down. I also added that if we got it launched properly, we could end up running all our own transportation instead of relying on others, who always took such a big slice of every shipment as a payment. That would mean earning even more cash.

She paused again before saying I should handle the DRWA end of the operation and insisting she didn't need to go there at this stage. I suspected she was scared of travelling to Africa. Underneath that tough exterior, she was still very much the spoilt daughter of a multi-millionaire drug baron. I could have insisted she travelled to the DRWA but then realized it was better not to have her with me. I could control the entire operation much more easily if she wasn't around.

Afterwards, I asked her if she was okay about it all.

"I'm fine," she said, slightly hesitantly.

When people say they're "fine" that usually means the exact opposite.

Another silence followed which was quite unnerving, but she broke it finally by asking: "Do you trust these Africans?"

"To a degree," I answered.

"What does that mean?" she asked.

"Like any new business, we have to iron out all the trust issues and then bed in properly, but I'm sure it will work out."

"Fair enough," she said, looking directly into my eyes before sticking her hand out awkwardly for me to shake.

"I guess we have a deal, partner," she said.

After the agreement, we celebrated by ordering room service and watching TV for the rest of that day.

The following morning, she got up early and left for the airport before I'd woken up. I didn't hurry to get out of bed and lay there agonizing about what I'd just got myself into. I kept telling myself I was doing the DRWA deal to help rescue my father from his gambling debts. But if I was going to be honest with myself, that wasn't the only reason.

In truth, I had no idea what to really expect in the DRWA. I'd gone against all my earlier instincts and walked back into the drug game. If all I was really looking for was a hit of excitement, then I'd chosen a very risky way to satisfy my cravings.

Within a week of that meeting in London, I was on a flight to the DRWA via Lagos to start setting up the African operation. I still kept telling myself I was doing this to help save my father's life, but I knew it might well end up costing me mine.

ACT III

ENDGAME

2002-2019

CHAPTER TWENTY
NARCO-STATE

Three armed men in suits in a Mercedes collected me at the chaotic, ramshackle airport on the outskirts of DRWA's capital city. As we swept out of the airport perimeter, we clipped an old lady, who was pushing a rusting shopping trolley, as she tried to cross the road in front of us. No one inside the car mentioned it and I was the only person to bother to turn round to see her sprawled out on the blistering blacktop. I was about to say she was hurt, when I noticed the eyes of the driver in the rear-view mirror watching me and thought better of it. I had what I thought were good reasons for agreeing to run the DRWA operation in the first place, although that didn't make it any easier to accept how cheap life really was inside that troubled nation.

As we sped through the crowded city streets that morning, I was told by the president's men to only use people recommended by the government. This included certain hand-picked units of soldiers, all of whom would expect a "tip" every time I used their services.

They eventually dropped me at a large, detached house in a gated community close to the capital's diplomatic district.

This was to be my home and came complete with five full-time staff, including my own driver. It felt from the start that I was being watched 24 hours a day to make sure I didn't do anything outside my "remit".

My most crucial task was to organize the construction of makeshift airstrips on the flatlands between the capital and the coast. All this had to be done out of sight of the city's resident NGOs as well as the NATO forces who regularly came through the DRWA en route to other African trouble spots.

The land for each airstrip had to be levelled out using old-fashioned colonial-era steam rollers to make them safe and long enough to land a large aircraft. The plan was that after no more than three shipments had been dropped off, we'd plough up each strip with mechanical diggers to make sure there was no evidence we'd ever been there in the first place. After all, this was the first time a small African nation had been transformed into a transport hub for the arrival and distribution of tens of millions of dollars' worth of drugs every month. Secrecy was of the utmost importance.

In late 2002 – just a couple of months after I arrived in the DRWA – a 40-year-old one-time Pan Am Boeing 707 airliner flew over from Chile packed to the rafters with cocaine and cannabis, hidden in boxes of chilies and bananas. The 707 had been purchased in South America for less than $100,000. It had then been filled with fuel. The toxic fumes of the cannabis inside the plane were so strong the pilots had to wear masks to avoid becoming disorientated.

La Princesa and her team of crooked accountants had calculated that it wasn't economically viable to fly the old workhorse planes back to South America after a drop-off because the cost of the fuel was more than the aircraft was worth. After unloading its cargo, the plane was taxied to the edge of the makeshift airstrip and pushed by a tractor into a local swamp nose first, where it sank slowly to the point where only the tip of its tailfin was visible. I knew that within a few hours that would be submerged too.

I remember watching it slowly disappearing as I stood there in my newly acquired bullet-proof vest thinking this was pretty serious stuff. I was thousands of miles from home in a strange, inhospitable land with no friends and surrounded by a bunch of untrustworthy characters, who'd shoot me at the drop of a hat if I stepped out of line.

How had it come to this? I felt like I was still an idealistic hippy at heart, yet here I was in the heart of darkness taking unimaginable risks. I couldn't help then thinking about how it all started: the storm, the boat and the cargo that may or may not have been there. The cargo that I still had no clues about.

* * *

Following that first successful delivery of drugs, two large planes began arriving in the DRWA each month loaded with

Chilean cocaine and cannabis worth a combined street value of at least $10 million. The produce was swiftly unloaded and split into smaller shipments to be transported by boat, plane and road up to Europe and beyond. I'd agreed with La Princesa that I would take a 1 per cent fee from the street value of each shipment. This meant I stood to earn at least $100,000 each time an aircraft safely landed in the DRWA and unloaded its cargo.

We had DRWA army units at our disposal, and this certainly helped when it came to running a smooth, trouble-free operation. The soldiers continued constructing new landing strips, clearing tracks through the jungle, and even built jetties deep into the swamp, so our boats could get as near as possible to where the planes landed to pick up the produce.

I kept La Princesa fully informed of all transactions on a secure satellite cell phone. She'd agreed that we shouldn't meet up until I got the operation properly up and running. She was clearly still not keen on visiting the DRWA, and it wasn't until we'd completed the first dozen runs from Chile without incident that she suggested meeting somewhere close to DRWA.

Then we hit some unforeseen problems.

* * *

All incoming aircraft checked in by radio transmitter with me when they were approaching the DRWA's Atlantic coastline as a security measure, in case there were any unforeseen problems in and around whatever airfield they were scheduled to land on. However, the day after my conversation with La Princesa, the crew on one of her rust-bucket 707s radioed in ahead of schedule to inform me their aircraft had suffered a double engine failure as it was about to enter local airspace. This left it with only two engines working, which meant that landing on our latest bespoke makeshift strip would be extremely risky.

I advised the pilots to head to a little-used, half-built airport in the south of the country, even though it was close to a large town, which meant the locals would probably see the plane arriving. We'd earlier promised the president's people this wouldn't happen, as he was paranoid about his citizens knowing what we were doing in their country, but there seemed nothing else to do.

After informing the crew, the 707 circled to dump excess fuel in the ocean. I called La Princesa on the satellite phone to tell her what was happening. She sounded irritated from the moment I told her and insisted that the pilots land the plane on the makeshift airstrip away from any populated areas to avoid upsetting the president.

"But they'll almost certainly end up crashing because they need a longer strip to land on with two engines," I explained.

There was silence at the other end of the line. Then she said: "That's not our problem. We must not upset the president. It's more important than anything."

I could tell from the tone of her voice that she wouldn't change her mind. But I also didn't want the death of those two pilots on my conscience. There was only one solution. I pretended the reception on the phone was bad and let the line go dead, even though I could hear her on the other end demanding that I obey her orders. I knew it was a big risk and that I would be held responsible if anything happened to the produce. But I ignored her calls back and instructed the 707 crew to head to that proper landing strip at the half-built airport, and then I made my way there. As I drove through the jungle, the satellite phone rang over and over again. I knew it was her and ignored the calls.

After reaching the new airfield, I paid the staff to ensure a fire engine was on standby in case the 707 broke up on landing. The most risky part of the operation related to how much distance the aircraft would need to land, because it only had two engines to put into reverse thrust as a braking system.

As I watched the airliner approach in the distance, it seemed to be swaying from side to side and the two dead engines were still smoking from the burning fuel. Getting closer, the plane dipped alarmingly and almost skimmed the tops of the huge, tall palm trees in the forest next to the airport perimeter. If it did crash, then it would all be on me.

The 707 finally touched down with a huge bump and bounced back up into the air twice before scraping along the tarmac as the pilots forced the two functioning engines into full reverse thrust. The noise was so loud it must have been heard from miles away. It eventually slewed to a halt on the edge of a deep swamp at the end of the only runway. Some local helpers and I drove out to the aircraft with a truck and quickly unloaded the produce while the fire engine smothered the two smoking engines with foam. The two pilots were understandably shaken but none the worse for wear and that evening headed back to Chile to live another day.

I had that 707 extra carefully dismantled and destroyed, as well as bribing the airport staff not to tell anyone what they'd seen.

* * *

Alongside me in the DRWA, I had two full-time gang members from the Chilean cartel. We actually went out of our way to keep apart from each other outside work hours, and I presumed they had no idea about my affair with their boss. But there were occasions when I knew they were keeping an eye on me for her.

A couple of days after the emergency landing, La Princesa called me in a fury and said that if I ever defied her like that again then we were finished. I didn't ask her to elaborate on whether that also meant we were no longer an item. Only a few days earlier, she'd told me she missed me and wanted to meet somewhere near the DRWA.

We never spoke about the incident again, although it was a reminder that the drugs came before anything else in her world. There was no mention of meeting again for the time being, either. I didn't know whether to feel relieved or bereft because my feelings for her were so conflicted. However, I didn't linger on all this for long because in a chaotic environment like the DRWA there are always plenty of things happening. I had to keep my wits about me at all times of the day and night. If something didn't feel right then I'd change my routine and spend a few days sussing out situations until, hopefully, any apparent danger passed.

The emergency landing at that airport had put me on a heightened state of alert that our presence in the DRWA might be exposed. There were rumours that one of the biggest Colombian cartels was looking for an "anchor point" in this part of Africa, so keeping a low profile in the DRWA remained a huge priority. It was in my interests to maintain security at all costs.

I paid out regular under-the-counter bribes to customs officers at the DRWA's only international airport, so that I always got a heads-up if any South Americans arrived in the country. I couldn't trust the president and his men to do this in case they were ever tempted to set up a new deal with one of our competitors.

As a result, I heard immediately when two Colombian men arrived in the DRWA about six months after we'd set up our operation there. They were booked in for a couple of nights at one of the capital's best hotels. I had been expecting this kind of situation to arise and so had a plan waiting in place. It began with a series of anonymous phone call threats to the Colombians pointing out that they were being watched and that it would be better if they pulled out of the DRWA.

The following morning the entire area around the hotel was cordoned off when a suspect package arrived at the hotel reception for the Colombians. It appeared to be a bomb, and the army had to be called in to organize a controlled explosion inside the hotel, which caused extensive damage but no loss of life. My contact inside the hotel later told me the Colombians departed on the next available flight out of the DRWA having concluded that it was not a safe enough environment in which to run their business.

The visit by those two Colombians was certainly a wake-up call, though. They were right to conclude it was a dangerous place. No wonder the president had dug me up to turn his little nation into a narco-state.

Our DRWA smuggling operation suffered no more direct problems following that one glitch when the 707's old engines blew out. We opened a warehouse on the outskirts of the capital under the pretext that it was part of a wind turbine investment corporation. It was guarded by local army and police around the clock. It was an ideal building for us to store our drugs safely and then transport them in smaller, more profitable loads. It also gave us an opportunity to further cut our cocaine with milk powder and laxative, a move that would potentially further triple our profits. It was around this time that many cocaine handlers across the globe began cutting cocaine much more than before. It became clear that users would still buy the drug, even if the real cocaine content was lowered to somewhere between 20 and 25 per cent.

The cocaine was repackaged inside tins and boxes of food, which would be relatively easy to smuggle out of the country, often in small aircraft. The cannabis coming in from Chile was usually taken by road, rail or ship north, as it was more bulky. But in the end, all of our drugs would eventually reach Europe and beyond. We often changed the type of transport out of the DRWA for shipments, so that if there were any leaks or security problems, we'd only end up having to shut down one route at a time. This would mean a minimal effect on our profits.

The most important thing for us was that by this time the majority of our "customers" were regulars, mainly from Europe and the UK, whom we could rely on to pay on time. They also took responsibility for the product from the moment they picked it up from whatever port, airfield or beach we'd transported it to, so we'd be able to take our second 50 per cent and move on swiftly to the next deal.

Ultimately, the DRWA was purely a transit point for our narcotics. There was no point in any of our drugs being sold on the streets there as virtually no one could afford to buy narcotics because they were so poor. This made our operation even more discrete – as well as efficient – when it came to anyone knowing what we were doing inside the country. Believing we weren't responsible for turning anyone in the DRWA into a drug addict did make it easier for me to deal with what we were doing there. But then something happened which turned that on its head.

The two Chileans who worked with me at the warehouse we owned in the centre of the city informed me that small quantities of cocaine had gone missing from three consecutive loads. It wasn't enough to concern us about loss of money, but we knew it meant one of the locals at the warehouse must have been responsible and we didn't want our product out on the streets because then people might start asking awkward questions. So we installed a micro-camera surveillance system covering the area where our drugs were always stored inside the warehouse and made sure all the local workers heard about it in the hope that the thief would stop stealing our produce. It worked perfectly, because no more drugs disappeared and we hadn't needed to reprimand anyone.

But a couple of weeks after this, the mother of one of our local workers turned up at the warehouse demanding to see me. At first, I was extremely reluctant to talk to her because we had expressly avoided contact with anyone outside our small workforce, as part of our agreement with the president and his men. However, she refused to leave the warehouse until I spoke to her. She told me through floods of tears that she'd just come from the city morgue after her son had been found dead in an alleyway from what his friends were saying was a cocaine overdose. They'd told the mother that her son had stolen the drugs from our warehouse. I denied all knowledge of any drugs as I tried to calm the woman down. In the end, we paid her off on the understanding that she'd keep quiet about what had happened to her son.

It was the first time we'd had such a tragic incident on our doorstep in the DRWA, and I for one felt really bad about it. The confrontation with the mother had naturally left a lot of bad karma in the air, so I knew immediately it wouldn't be the last we'd be hearing about it.

Three days after the mother's visit to the warehouse, four men in masks carrying automatic weapons forced their way into the warehouse just as the two Chileans were locking up for the evening. There was a firefight and all four of the locals were shot by the Chileans. One of the raiders lived just long enough to admit to the Chileans that the same mother had sold them information about the cocaine being smuggled through the warehouse.

We'd just exterminated four locals and no doubt word of our operation would be spreading fast in the ghetto. We could end up a sitting target. The bodies of the four men were loaded onto a truck and secretly buried out in the countryside. I immediately found another warehouse on the other side of the city, and we moved our operation there and employed a new workforce.

The shootings were a clear warning sign about the dangers we were facing in the DRWA, though. But I didn't tell La Princesa what had happened because I was worried she might blame me if we had any subsequent problems. I even managed to persuade the two Chileans not to tell her, either. They seemed relieved not to.

Months passed, and with the DRWA operation seemingly running itself by this time, despite those earlier teething problems, my friendship with La Princesa once again became more convivial. I encouraged her to believe our personal relationship could continue and told myself I'd done that because I didn't want to do anything to upset her. Our earlier row was never mentioned.

The conversations between us were often punctuated at this time by admissions that we missed each other. So, despite some reservations, I agreed to meet her on the Spanish island of Tenerife, the perfect under-the-radar holiday destination off the coast of West Africa. I was desperate for some one-on-one contact with someone after many months of isolation in the DRWA.

The following weekend, La Princesa arrived in Tenerife on a scheduled flight from Madrid, and I managed to hitch a ride on one of the president's fleet of Lear jets. We'd agreed not to meet at Tenerife's main airport, in case anyone was monitoring either or both of us. So we arrived at different times at a hotel she'd booked on one of the island's biggest holiday resorts. It turned out to be jam packed with mainly British tourists, who'd arrived on the island to soak up some winter sunshine.

La Princesa was on the balcony of the suite when I arrived at the room. I joined her and we watched hundreds of noisy, drunk tourists cavorting around the pool area and awkwardly exchanged pleasantries about our flights. We were both testing the water with each other. After a glass of wine, I asked her in passing what her life was like back in Chile. She seemed taken aback and would only say "It's fine" and then changed the subject.

The odd thing was that my initial reluctance to jump straight in probably helped us feel more connected to each other that first day in Tenerife. Whatever our relationship was, there was a twisted sense of neediness running through it. So I ignored her flat response to my question about life in Chile and suggested we get all the work stuff out of the way and then have dinner together. But then a lot of our happiness with each other was down to the financial success of the operation. While it was going well, it was like an aphrodisiac in some ways.

I began the work stuff by discussing the need to step up the size of the shipments, so that we could increase earnings enough to pull out of the DRWA before any of the bigger cartels made a move. She told me to relax and not worry because she envisaged the operation continuing for many years. Still keen to push for a "withdrawal plan", I took the plunge and mentioned the raid on the warehouse. It was a stupid move because she was immediately irritated that I hadn't told her about it at the time it occurred. In the end, we agreed to disagree about when to pull out of the DRWA. She continued to insist we wouldn't be doing so for a long time to come.

After we'd wrapped up the business side of things, we ordered a room-service dinner and ended up sharing a bottle of wine. But after the second glass she refused my offer of a refill, which surprised me.

"It's good to keep a clear head sometimes," she said.

"Why do you need to keep a clear head?" I asked.

"Because there are things we need to talk about."

"Okay," I said, hesitantly.

"I need to know how you feel about us," she said.

Yet again I was lost for words.

"I love you although I know you're still unsure about me," she whispered.

I didn't know what to say but before I had a chance to respond, she added: "What if you discovered that we shared a mutual love for someone very special. Would that make a difference to how you feel about me?"

I sensed immediately she was talking about La Patrona.

"It's time to be completely honest with you," she said.

She told me she'd slept with La Patrona in Madrid and they'd fallen in love. But then she'd become angry with her for not having the courage to tell her father, the cartel chief at the time, that they were in a relationship. After they'd had a huge row about it, La Patrona went to the cartel chief and naïvely told him there was someone else in her life in the hope he'd end their relationship and she could then be with his daughter. But the father's machismo wouldn't let it rest after she told him. He was so affronted by not having her to himself that he tortured La Patrona to try and find out who her secret lover was. But she wouldn't say, so he never realized it was his own daughter.

"She died protecting me," said La Princesa. "But it feels like I pulled the trigger."

"You can't blame yourself," I said, computing everything she'd just told me. She looked genuinely heartbroken and I wasn't shocked because my own mother had been close to other women in the past.

"I was just a simple, hard-working student with aspirations to be a doctor. But by killing her, my father turned me into a cold-blooded person. I hate myself for being like this."

She paused for a moment.

"My father killed not only the person I thought I loved more than anyone else in the world, but he also killed the person I was so desperate to be. I wanted him to suffer because of that."

Was she saying she'd had her own father killed? Did she give the information to the old chief about her father's plans, which led to his death? I put my arms around her and held her tight to try and comfort her while these questions went through my head. I understood her pain, but I was also trying to play for time.

If I survived long enough, I'd need to look at my own character defects more closely to try and understand why I ignored so many obvious flags about La Princesa. Maybe it all went back to my mother and the way her experiences impacted on my upbringing? Her character had been so extreme (and unique) that I seemed prepared to welcome even the most troubled people into my life.

It was only then I noticed that she wasn't wearing the bracelet I'd bought her during our shopping trip in Madrid. I was tempted to ask her why, but it wasn't the right time or place, so I closed my eyes. Maybe it was better to just sleep, or pretend to at least.

I kept one eye on her throughout the night and decided to bite my lip and act as if everything was perfectly normal. Whatever was really going on, I needed to keep the relationship going, because sometimes you have to make huge sacrifices in order to find out the truth.

CHAPTER TWENTY-ONE
TARGETED

In the DRWA, a large delegation of Chinese construction workers and engineers were constantly travelling in and out of the country, which added to the edgy atmosphere because you could never be absolutely sure what they were really up to. The Chinese presence seemed to be centred around the building of a pan-African highway to transport all the minerals they'd started plundering from inside the DRWA and other surrounding African nations. Their highway was intended to link Africa's west and east coasts so that everything could then be loaded onto ships to be transported to China.

But I knew their existence in the DRWA would attract even more curious "onlookers", which once again could lead to the exposure of the Chilean cartel's operation. When you're in a criminal mindset, as I was at that time, these are the sorts of things that constantly go through your head.

It was obvious the Chinese didn't want to upset the DRWA president, who was in their pocket as well. The Chinese were even helping him launder a lot of his excess cash through a myriad of money exchange businesses located across Africa and Asia.

The president's "tax" paid by the Chinese and our narco cash should have helped transform the lives of millions of DRWA citizens by providing new schools, roads and other public amenities. But from what I saw, that wasn't happening.

While I was in the country, I continued to be shadowed by what I presumed were agents working for the president, rather than any foreign law enforcement organizations. I could have just asked him or his men why they were following me, but that was against the "rules" in my game. They wouldn't have admitted what they were doing anyway, and I couldn't afford to upset him.

Then something happened which convinced me to be a lot more careful about my movements. I'd got my driver to drop me in the centre of the city one evening and ended up alone in a dive bar, downing whisky shots and boring two local women about my life back in Ibiza. It was a stupid thing to do, but I'd been cooped up in the house and felt the need to escape for a few hours.

I remember looking across the bar as I chatted to the women and noticing two men glaring at me. There was nothing unusual about this in the DRWA because of an understandable tension between local residents and any of the "rich" Europeans who lived, like me, in the diplomatic district. But, fuelled up by alcohol, I ended up nodding at the two men in quite a flippant way. Not long after this, I started feeling very dizzy and fell off my bar stool. The last thing I remember was hitting the floor of the bar and looking up as two pairs of men's shoes came towards me.

I came round in an alleyway with the same shoes inches from my face. One of the men pulled me up and held me while the other smashed his fist into my stomach at least half a dozen times. Then they dragged me to a van waiting at the other end of the alleyway. Once inside it, one man started driving while the other one who'd punched me turned and looked at me over his shoulder from the front seat: "You're a lucky white man. You could have ended up dead in the gutter. Stay away from the locals. We won't tell you again."

The van arrived outside my house and one of the men pulled me out onto the roadway and then kicked me again for good measure. I stayed on the ground until their van moved off before struggling to my feet and stumbling into the house. It seemed that my presidential shadows were controlling every aspect of my life. I'd overstepped the mark, so they'd slipped me a Mickey Finn and then beaten me up to teach me a lesson. This was the world I now inhabited.

I felt a sense of even more severe isolation after that, trapped in my house or working in the warehouse unable to visit the real city in case I crossed the wrong people. I didn't actually blame the president for wanting to keep an eye on me, though. After all, I was a drug lord from a foreign country. He already knew a lot about my background through my connection with his son, and I'm sure that didn't instil confidence in my character.

He'd carefully avoided seeing me in person since I'd first encountered his men in London, but for me, the longer I didn't meet the president, the better. There were rumours that the Americans were monitoring him by satellite after fresh allegations that his troops had been executing their own citizens, including rival politicians. I heard from one local contact that my best friend had further fallen out with his father because of those alleged atrocities. I was so deeply immersed in our operation inside the country by this time that I had to put any feelings about my oldest friend to one side, though. I knew he'd be hurting to know what I was doing with his father, but I didn't have much choice in the matter.

If I suggested to the president that we wanted to pull out, not only would my life be in danger but he'd most likely immediately approach one of the bigger cartels to set up their operation inside the DRWA to replace us. Then I'd definitely be unable to get out of his country alive. I was convinced the only reason the president hadn't done any of this was because he knew that a bigger cartel might create a lot more attention and that they'd expect much more control over his country. We were the ideal companion, but not irreplaceable.

I would, however, get the occasional call from the president. He'd want to talk about his son, whom he admitted he hadn't seen for some years, but these conversations were really his way of reminding me I owed him another bribe. No doubt he was well aware that others were probably listening in to his phone conversations, so it was a way of checking in without directly addressing our business. Following his calls to me, his henchmen would usually sweep into the driveway of my detached home in a limousine to collect his cash.

The president was receiving somewhere in the region of $2 million a month from the cartel. A further $1 million was spread around his various political allies, armed services and police chiefs. There were also obligatory "tips" for the troops on the ground.

In addition to my permanent staff at the house, I had three armed guards round the clock by this time. The only large amounts of cash I kept at the house were for the bribes I was obliged to pay. However, I feared the president's rebel opposition or local criminals might raid the property to try and steal that cash, so we needed to be prepared.

When I wasn't stuck waiting for a rusty old airliner to touch down on a muddy makeshift airstrip at the dead of night or overseeing a drugs conveyor belt inside our warehouse on the edge of the capital, life in the DRWA had become even more mundane since my close shave in that bar. The only people I felt safe to mix with were a couple of European expats living near me in the diplomatic district of the city. I told them I was setting up wind farms across Africa. I'd even registered the wind farm investment business as a proper company by this stage and opened an office in the city centre employing a staff of three locals in addition to the warehouse.

Half a dozen wind turbines would eventually be erected in plain sight along the coast at a cost of $1 million each to prove the company was legitimate. They also turned out to be ideal flight path locators for the old airliners flying in from Chile. The millions invested in those wind turbines was only a tiny fraction of the cash the cartel was earning by this time, so we saw these purchases as an affordable expense.

* * *

Over this period, I only spoke occasionally to La Princesa on the phone because we'd agreed to maintain "radio silence" unless there were any problems with the operation. She'd long since stopped saying she missed me, but I still harboured hopes we might meet again in somewhere like Tenerife.

However, after four or five months of just the occasional snatched conversation about the business, I did wonder if something had happened to her in Chile. The last time we'd been together was when she'd confessed about her love for La Patrona and her father's murder. What she'd said had rocked me to the core, but I knew I had to keep those feelings to myself while I continued to work for the cartel.

I didn't want her thinking I was in any way angry with her, because then she might get ideas about ending our partnership permanently.

My satellite phone rang one morning and her number came up on the screen. I felt quite relieved to be hearing from her and answered it after just one ring. But she wasn't on the other end of the line. It was one of her henchmen. He sounded tense and ignored my question about where she was before informing me that the cartel was going to increase the size of the loads, so I needed to double up on security my end. It was very awkward because I couldn't press him about where she was, without giving away any hints about our relationship. Just before the call ended, I asked the henchman if he could get La Princesa to call me. He never responded and the line went dead.

I rang back at least a dozen times over the following few days and left messages for her. But when I didn't hear anything back, I started to wonder if maybe I should feel quite relieved that we seemed not to be speaking anymore. At least that meant we hadn't had to end it acrimoniously. So I accepted the situation and stopped trying to phone her. I even became more relaxed with her henchman in Chile, who continued calling me from her phone to discuss business. He made it clear it was very much work as usual, even though it didn't feel the same as before.

But I got increasingly unnerved by La Princesa's absence because there were still many unanswered questions, including the biggest one of all about when to quit the DRWA. I remained convinced it had to be sooner rather than later.

Over the following month or so, I got a bit closer to the two Chileans working with me at our warehouse. I'd accepted that they were most likely reporting stuff back to the cartel, but I had nothing to hide, so I didn't really care. One of them was particularly chatty, and one day we were having lunch inside the warehouse when he actually opened up a bit about his life back in Chile.

I eventually worked the conversation round to La Princesa's life in Chile. What was her house like? Did she have a lot of friends?

"Friends?" replied the Chilean. "No, but she likes men, that's for sure."

"Really?" I asked.

"She went a bit *loco* (mad) after her father died. But she's calmed down now and got married," said the Chilean, hesitating, probably because he realized he'd already said too much.

I stopped eating mid-mouthful and poured us both some water from a jug on the table.

"Married, eh?" I said.

"Yeah, poor guy doesn't know what he's let himself in for," said the Chilean. "She's one tough cookie."

He looked across at me as he said it, so I quickly changed the subject and went back to talking about our operation in the DRWA.

Her being married certainly made sense, though. She'd reacted defensively when I'd earlier pressed her about her life back in Chile. She also hadn't been wearing that bracelet I'd bought for her the last time I'd seen her.

One side of me definitely felt humiliated to hear she'd got married. It felt like I'd been ditched without an explanation. My pride was deeply hurt, even though I'd always had so many reservations about her. Maybe everything she'd told me had been a lie, from being abused by her father to her role in the death of La Patrona?

I was overwhelmed with self-doubt during the first couple of hours after I found out La Princesa was married. Eventually, I snapped myself out of it and concluded that her marriage was a blessing in disguise because it meant all the pain and doubt connected to her and our affair was finally over. But none of this stopped it being one massive mindfuck, though.

Over the following few days, I tried to compute the situation by going over some key questions. What would she do next? Did her marriage mean I was expendable? Or did she intend on continuing our affair behind the back of her husband? I needed to get a grip on what was happening. I couldn't afford to take my eye off the ball, especially when

I thought back to how my boss had melted down and it had eventually cost him his life.

At the warehouse, the chatty Chilean and I had become new best friends. One day he asked me if I thought all the dust from the cocaine and laxative we used to "stretch" the product was dangerous to ingest. It was a strange question, since we'd been handling mountains of coke for almost two years by this stage. He insisted he only mentioned it because he knew a couple of men back in Chile who'd recently ended up with cancer after handling vast amounts of cocaine.

I asked him what happened to them. He seemed uncomfortable about my question at first, but then revealed that La Princesa's husband was one of those men. He'd recently been diagnosed with lung cancer. Now I realized why she'd stopped calling me. Was it possible the Chilean had deliberately leaked that information to me after orders from her? It could have been her way of ending our relationship.

At the end of the day, I should have been relieved to know what was going on with her, but I was also quite disorientated by yet another deception. I'd enjoyed meeting her in Tenerife. It had been good for my sanity, or so I thought. But I couldn't say any of this to her. It was far too risky. As this realization dawned on me, I felt more lonely than I'd ever felt before in my entire life.

I began spending most of my spare time locked up in the house watching old movies. Sometimes I'd have one too many beers and pull out my satellite phone and punch out her number but not actually call her. Her marriage had got to me in a way I hadn't expected. The nights were even worse, though. I'd lie in bed for hours going through everything she'd told me in my head. Then I'd get even more angry with myself for still feeling connected to her, despite everything that had happened.

I eventually decided I needed to get out and about more. It would also make me less suspicious to the other foreigners living in the DRWA capital. I knew that as long as I stuck to the Europeans who lived in my neighbourhood, then the president and his men probably wouldn't object.

As a "wind farm entrepreneur", I managed to get myself on the list for the DRWA's diplomatic cocktail party circuit, which centred around embassies and diplomatic residences near my home. The first one I attended was a Bastille Day reception at the French Embassy. I didn't know if anyone suspected what I was really doing in the DRWA, but no one confronted me. Some people were full of praise for the school and road projects that my wind turbines would hopefully help to power one day.

About halfway through the evening, I met a Swiss woman who worked for an NGO. Initially, I was suspicious she might be a plant, because we seemed to click very easily after a conversation about how little there was to do in the DRWA.

By the end of that same evening, though, I was convinced we had a genuine connection, so I asked her out on a date.

We saw each other four or five times over the following month. It was refreshing to have a relationship with a "normal" person I could talk to about stuff that didn't revolve around drug deals and crooked politicians. I began calling her my girlfriend, and we went to bars and restaurants frequented mainly by Europeans. What I didn't realize at the time was that someone was taking photographs of us as we walked around holding hands.

She eventually spent the weekend at my house, and we both acknowledged that the relationship was getting much more serious. We talked about maybe living together in the countryside outside the capital. She made a point of saying that her bosses as well as her parents back in Geneva would approve of her living with a respectable, middle-aged wind farm entrepreneur.

On the Sunday evening, she left my house to go to her own home for the evening because she wanted to prepare for an important NGO meeting the following morning. I remember kissing her in the driveway before she got in her car and noticing a couple of men sitting in a jeep up the street. But it didn't bother me, because I was used to the president's men keeping an eye on me.

Half an hour later, I called her to make sure she'd got home safely, but there was no answer. I gave it another 30 minutes and called again. But she still wasn't picking up. Not long after that, her boss at the NGO called me to say she'd been car-jacked. Two men in a jeep had forced her vehicle off a road on the outskirts of the capital. She'd been dragged out of the vehicle and shot in the head twice. She died at the scene.

Before he'd even finished telling me the details, I wondered if she'd been specifically targeted. After the call, I became overcome with a toxic combination of grief and guilt. Grief because in such a short time we'd had a close relationship. Guilt because I was convinced her murder had to be connected to me.

For at least half an hour, I paced up and down in the sitting room of my house trying to work out what to do next. In the end, I threw caution to the wind and headed out to my car, insisting to my duty driver that I would get behind the wheel myself. I drove straight to the city police headquarters to demand a proper explanation. I knew it was a risky thing to do because my presence was sure to prompt some awkward questions about who I was and why I was in the DRWA.

The duty officer at the headquarters insisted I wait in the reception area while he tried to get hold of one of the detectives investigating the murder. Almost immediately, two of the president's men appeared in the hallway of the building. They told me I had to leave. At first I refused, but then both of them took my arms and ushered me outside, despite my protests.

As we stood in the deserted car park at the back of the building, they warned me not to go to the police station ever again because they didn't want questions being asked about who I really was. I shook them off me and told them to fuck off. But instead of giving me a kicking like last time, they stood by my car and waited for me to get in and drive away. If I hadn't left, they'd probably have shot me there and then.

I drove back to my house completely shattered by what had happened and hating the fact I felt so fucking impotent. Not only had someone died because they were close to me, but I couldn't tell anyone my suspicions or do anything about it.

Back at the house that night, my girlfriend's boss rang me again and began asking some much more inquisitive questions about my job in the DRWA. I offered my condolences and ended the call as quickly as I could without appearing to be impolite.

I tried to get some sleep that night, but it was impossible. At about 3 a.m., I got up to make myself a honey and lemon drink to soothe my nerves when La Princesa phoned me after months of silence. She asked how I was and said she was missing me. Before I could respond, the phone line went dead.

I presumed she'd call back, but she never did. I had many questions to ask her about her husband and whether she had a connection to the murder of my girlfriend.

Despite my conflicting emotions and a feeling of responsibility for what had happened to them, I couldn't let anything impact the operation, so I soldiered on.

* * *

And there were other problems mounting on the horizon in the DRWA. My best friend's gloomy prediction that his own father would become the ultimate African tyrant was proving correct, with allegations of more atrocities being reported in the media across the globe. It was obvious that as the outcry against him grew, he'd become much more dangerous. I became concerned that there would be international intervention against his regime, and that if he went down our operation would be destroyed with him.

Opposition politicians inside DRWA alleged that building projects and road construction had been shelved after the president and his cronies dipped into the aid payments for themselves. This was backed up by the very blatant construction of a vast new gold-leaf-lined presidential mansion on the outskirts of the capital. It had been specifically designed to look like the Palace of Versailles. By this time, the president also openly admitted to having 32 children by numerous wives. No wonder his son – my best friend – wouldn't talk to him anymore.

In the middle of all this, the president responded to his many critics by appointing a tall, balding former Chechen arms dealer as his new personal assistant. This man apparently had a direct line to Russian president Vladimir Putin, who was said to be eyeing up the lucrative mineral reserves in the north of the country, which had already caught the attention of the Chinese. The same character was rumoured to be connected to a Chechen drug cartel, so naturally we became concerned. I'd been half expecting the Colombians to make a return visit since that earlier trip to the DRWA, but now the most imminent threat was actually coming from a shadowy figure reputed to be the leader of a gang of trigger-happy ex-special forces soldiers.

The president's latest moves made it clear he wanted even more bribes to be paid to him. He nationalized the DRWA's biggest silver mine after it had been in the ownership of a Belgian company for almost a hundred years. It was alleged that the president had kicked them out after they refused to pay him larger bribes.

The silver mine was soon attracting yet more illicit payments for the president and his people from Western companies in exchange for being granted licences to work there. I could tell we'd soon lose our influence with him as other, bigger pay-masters circled. I tried to call La Princesa to tell her what was happening, but she wasn't picking up her satellite phone again.

Meanwhile, the streets of the capital were getting increasingly dangerous, as large numbers of citizens began talking about mounting a revolt against their corrupt leader. Armed troops were roaming the city policing a curfew that the president hoped would quell all public protests against him.

* * *

In the middle of all this, La Princesa seemed to have completely disappeared. I didn't know whether to rejoice at this fact or wait for the ultimate knock on the door.

About a month after my NGO girlfriend's murder, I was enduring yet another sleepless night at the house when I received a call from La Princesa's satellite phone number. I didn't answer it at first because I presumed it was her henchman again since she'd not returned any of my earlier calls.

The caller rang back three times in succession, so I eventually answered it to be greeted by a long beat of silence and just the sound of someone breathing heavily. Then La Princesa came on the line. Her voice sounded flat and business-like. Why would I have expected anything else?

I had so many things to ask her, but she headed straight into the "game" by clinically telling me she'd just accepted 50 per cent upfront from one of our biggest European customers, for a large load of cocaine which would arrive from Chile later that week. She didn't once ask how I was. I had to instantly decide whether to play it her way or try to take the conversation in a different direction.

"There's a lot of shit going down here. Sending a shipment now would be a big mistake," I finally said, ignoring all the other stuff on my mind.

"The deal's already done. I can't change it."

"But…"

"It's too late. It's on its way."

I should have confronted her with the threat of the Chechens and everything else that was happening in the DRWA. But it was clear she didn't give a flying fuck. As ever, money ruled her world above all else.

My paranoid criminal mindset, which I kept in check most of the time, came into play. I didn't want her to think I would disappear, but I also suspected she might be planning to turn me into the ultimate sacrificial lamb by stranding me in the DRWA while she pulled her operation out of Africa unscathed. If I did end up stuck there, then I wouldn't last long. If I left without paying up all the bribes the president was owed, he'd have me arrested and imprisoned before I even got outside the capital. Then I'd most likely be executed to stop me talking about our narco-state arrangement.

Her voice never changed its flat tone throughout that phone call. She sounded almost as if she was reading everything from a script. I didn't mention that or her husband, although I was convinced he was listening in to our conversation.

I should have known what was coming next.

A few minutes after the call ended, the normally quiet, tree-lined street in front of my government-supplied house erupted as thousands of anti-president protestors descended on the diplomatic district of the city. Just a few miles away, a group of rebels kidnapped half a dozen politicians belonging to the president's party and executed them for accepting bribes. Many of them had been on the cartel's payroll.

There was a feeling of pressure and fear mounting throughout the city. On one side, I had a greedy, murderous tyrant and on the other was a duplicitous, two-timing cartel boss, who'd always made it clear to me where her ultimate priorities really lay.

* * *

The morning after that phone call from La Princesa, my NGO girlfriend's boss called me again. His voice sounded much less sympathetic and more controlled this time.

"What is it you actually do here?" he asked me after we'd exchanged pleasantries.

I explained once again about the wind turbines, but he didn't seem to be listening.

"Did you know she was in danger?" he said.

I wanted to tell him the truth. I was sick of hiding stuff. Maybe it was time to make a clean sweep of it all. She hadn't deserved to die, and yes, it was my fault. I took a long deep breath and remembered something the Brit once told me right at the start of my criminal career. He said: "The best lies are the ones that are the nearest to the truth."

So I told her boss: "I wish I knew why she died. If I could do anything that would help bring her back I'd do it, I really would."

It was the truth in a roundabout sort of way. I ended the call by claiming I was late for a meeting and promising to ring him back later.

The way her boss had inferred I was to blame for her death shook me to the core. A dark sense of guilt and doom overwhelmed me after I spoke to him. I needed to take some long deep breaths, get a grip of the situation and work out a survival strategy.

* * *

In the end, I decided it was essential to make sure that last shipment of cartel drugs made it out of the DRWA safely. Looking back on it now, I don't know why I had such a misplaced sense of loyalty to someone who by this stage clearly didn't give a fuck about me.

I was in the middle of trying to work out all the logistics for the incoming load when I was phoned by the New Zealander in Ibiza. He told me my mother had fallen down the stairs at her villa and broken her hip. The doctors were saying that she was very sick and that I needed to get back to the island immediately.

Hearing the news about my mother shook me up and I wrestled with it for hours. She was yet again looming over a pivotal moment in my life. She'd never been a mother in the traditional sense, but when I was growing up it had often felt as if it was us against the world, and I'd never fully shaken off that bond. If I'd asked her for advice at that very moment, she would no doubt have said something like: "Forget me and save your own neck."

Death and destruction would almost certainly occur if that last shipment didn't get delivered to the cartel's European client, which meant staying in the DRWA was undoubtedly the safer option, in the short-term. But what about my mother? It sounded like she was on her deathbed. The drugs underworld was controlling my fate and blurring my ability to see the wood for the trees.

Then I got a phone call at the house from the president's office. One of his staff informed me that he wanted me to meet with the president's new Chechen personal assistant the following afternoon to discuss some "new business". My mother would no doubt have said it sounded like a classic trap. All my hesitation about fleeing the DRWA dissolved in a nanosecond after that phone call ended. It really was now or never.

My escape would have to be swiftly and efficiently executed or else the president would have my head on a plate.

* * *

The key to getting away from the DRWA safely was to act normally. I couldn't make any big changes to my usual routine, otherwise that might flag up my intentions. So I sat tight until the following morning.

At precisely 10 a.m., I got my driver to take me to our warehouse as he always did. I tried to make light conversation with him as we weaved through the narrow streets towards the city centre. Often, my presidential shadows wouldn't bother following us to the warehouse because my driver was obliged to inform them of my movements. But when I looked behind us as we pulled off, I noticed the president's men on our tail. They weren't very subtle. Maybe the Chechen had ordered them to keep an especially close eye on me in case I bolted before I met him later that afternoon. But there was nothing I could do except keep going.

The crowds of protestors out on the streets that morning made the journey painfully slow. There were roadblocks everywhere and it was no surprise when we got stopped about a mile from the warehouse. Two of the policemen manning the roadblock looked tense as they approached our vehicle, but then they suddenly waved us on when my shadows in the car behind us flashed a card at one of the officers.

Eventually, my driver dropped me off outside the warehouse at exactly the same spot where he did every morning. Remember, maintaining my normal routine was crucial. I headed into the building and went straight to my first-floor office. Once there, I glanced down from a window to make sure my shadows had parked where they usually did out front.

But their car was nowhere to be seen. I looked around in all directions. Maybe they'd gone to get a coffee or something, safe in the knowledge that I'd be in the building for some time. Or perhaps they'd be waiting if I tried to slip out of the back of the empty warehouse as I was planning.

It was too risky to abandon my plan and try the following day, so I put a baseball cap on and grabbed a jacket I kept at the warehouse and headed for the emergency fire exit at the rear of the building. Once outside, I headed down a dusty alleyway into a nearby road. As I was calmly walking across it, I noticed the president's men in their car parked at the far end of the street. They'd sensibly chosen a vantage point where they could see anyone leaving the front and the back of the warehouse. The Chechen must have been behind that precaution.

Despite seeing them, I didn't hesitate and kept on walking. Thanks to the baseball cap, I could have been a local. I eventually darted into a maze of alleyways, which I knew led to a taxi rank. I got in the back of the second cab in a queue, checking carefully behind us in case my shadows had seen me and were following, but there was no sign of them.

The journey through the suburbs of the capital was surprisingly quiet, as the driver proudly informed me he knew all the back routes to avoid the crowds of protestors on the other side of the city.

About 20 miles from the capital, the cab dropped me at a ramshackle railway station. I paid the driver and went straight to the ticket office where I purchased a ticket into the capital. Then I walked onto the platform and waited for a train among a group of travellers and two policemen, who were watching me closely. After the train slowly ground to a halt, I got into an almost empty carriage and found a seating area with no one else around.

Just before the train moved off, I opened the carriage door on the other side and jumped onto the ground. I managed to find a gap in some bushes alongside the track and headed on to a dusty pathway that led into the centre of the town. Behind me the train was slowly moving off in the opposite direction.

I eventually found a taxi rank with five cabs on it and once again took the second one. An hour later, it arrived at the tightly controlled DRWA border with another impover-ished African neighbour state. At the crossing point, DRWA border officers checked and re-checked my fake passport over and over again until I realized they were waiting for a bribe. I should have known better.

After paying them, I began walking through the customs area when one of the border officers shouted at me to stop. I kept walking without looking back. Then I felt a hand on my shoulder and turned round. The same officer held on to me and pointed in front of us. Two of his colleagues had stopped a truck just inside the DRWA side of the border gate. They drew their guns and began shouting at the two men inside the vehicle. Two more DRWA border guards rushed to the other side of the truck, also with guns drawn. Three shots rang out moments later.

I was so transfixed by what was happening that when the customs officer who'd stopped me tapped my shoulder and pointed me in the direction of a pedestrian exit to the other side, I nearly jumped out of my skin.

As the bodies of the two men in the truck were dragged out of the vehicle, I headed towards the neighbouring country on the other side of the border crossing. Behind me, I heard the sirens of police cars approaching on the DRWA side. Walking through the gate, I turned and watched as the police cruisers skidded to a halt outside the DRWA customs post. As officers got out of the cars, I recognized the two president's men who'd been waiting outside the warehouse earlier.

As I walked down the road that led away from the customs post, I removed my baseball cap and turned round once again. I could see one of the president's men looking straight at me across the border. So I smiled and waved. After rounding the first corner of that road, I caught a taxi to the nearest international airport.

In this game, you often have to think on your feet. I'd planned to get out of the DRWA before anyone even realized I'd gone, but in the end it had been by the skin of my teeth.

CHAPTER TWENTY-TWO
UNDER THE RADAR

Twenty-four hours later, I arrived at the hospital in Ibiza to find my mother drifting in and out of consciousness. It was impossible to have a coherent conversation with her, so I simply smiled at her whenever she opened her eyes and held her hand as I sat next to her.

The doctor explained that not only had she broken her hip but her one good leg had got infected after the fall down the stairs. She'd also had a small stroke in the ambulance on the way to the hospital, so was in a very bad way.

She was exhausted and had been pumped full of medicine, so I decided it would be better if I came back the next morning.

* * *

I went to the airport that evening to pick up my father, who'd insisted on flying in when he heard about my mother. Despite them having been apart for more than 30 years, he was very upset. As we drove back to her villa, I tried to sympathize with him, but it was awkward, knowing what had happened in the past.

He warned me that I shouldn't go back to the DRWA. Although I already knew it, he told me it was about to be ripped apart by civil war. I pointed out that my earnings from the cartel had helped pay off all his gambling debts, as well as cancelling out those loans from the DRWA.

"You don't really have the right to lecture me," I said.

It was an awkward moment, when we should have been sharing our fears about my mother's health. It also brought him round to his favourite topic of all – my uncle. He insisted that all our problems were down to him. So I did what I should have done many years earlier and challenged him to explain what he really meant by that.

"Do you really want to know?" he asked.

"Yes."

Firstly, my father explained how he and my mother had met and fallen in love and married, and how happy they'd been until a few years later, when a man turned up on their doorstep in London, a man my mother claimed she had once been in love with.

"She thought this man was dead after he'd disappeared during the civil war," said my father. "I was in pieces. This complete stranger was threatening to destroy our happiness together."

But, my father explained to me, he knew that if he tried to stop her it would end up making them more likely to run off together.

"So I encouraged her to meet this man and decide for herself whom she wanted to spend the rest of her life with. I didn't want to do it, but I knew it was my only chance," he said.

They ended up sleeping together on the first night of that "reunion", but the very next day, my mother realized it had all been a terrible mistake because he wasn't the same man he'd been during the civil war. He'd turned into a brash, underworld henchman with a ruthless streak, who'd thrived in the post-war 1950s London underworld.

"She had a complete change of heart," explained my father. "And begged me to take her back. I didn't hesitate, because I loved her."

Then he paused for a moment.

"And you were born about nine months after all this happened."

I now knew for the first time what I'd long suspected – that my "uncle" wasn't my uncle at all, but my real father. It certainly helped explain a lot of the stuff that had happened since, as well as the clear physical similarities between us, which I'd always tried to ignore. My father told me he'd agreed to allow my uncle to occasionally see me when I was growing up as long as he didn't tell me he was my real father. No wonder my father decided he'd had enough after my mother took me to see my uncle in prison. He must have realized at that moment that she was still in love with him, despite everything.

"As far as I'm concerned, you're my real father and always will be," I told him after he'd finished.

My father smiled with relief at having got it all off his chest.

* * *

The next morning, I went with my father to see my mother in hospital, and this time she was surprisingly coherent and delighted to see both of us. We all spoke fondly about the past for about half an hour, although it did seem awkward at times after what my father had just told me.

Then, as we all sat in silence for a few moments, I took the plunge and mentioned what he'd said to me the previous night. My father looked mortified that I was unravelling it all, but I was determined to finally get it all out in the open. When I'd finished, my mother smiled and said she was relieved I finally knew the truth and thanked my father for telling me.

"You should have told me all this yourself," I said, trying to be gentle about it because of her condition.

"Ich weib. Ich weib (I know. I know)," she whispered in German, which had always been our secret language when we didn't want my father – or anyone else for that matter – to know what we were talking about. I immediately switched back to English out of respect for my father, but she continued speaking German and said it had been very hard for him and he had every right to be angry.

My father looked infuriated, stood up and left the room. My mother asked me in German not to try and stop him because there was something she wanted to tell me which concerned my uncle. It had been a source of deep regret to her ever since the civil war.

She said it all came to a head after she'd read that Hollywood director's outline of her story on that day at the beach. It had inspired her to reveal the truth to my "uncle" about how they'd really broken out from that prison camp. They had only got away because she'd slept with one of the guards so that he would look the other way while they escaped. My mother said my uncle was stunned but insisted she tell him who that guard was. She admitted it was the old Guardia Civil chief, who'd been in the beach bar with them just a few minutes earlier. My mother even made a point of saying to my uncle that afternoon that she didn't hate the police chief for what he did to her because without his help they would never have escaped.

But, she told me, she immediately regretted telling my uncle. He accused her of betraying him, even though she'd done it to save both their lives. It was only then she realized his anger was because she'd taken something very personal away from him.

"He'd always thought he'd been the one who got us out of that prison camp," said my mother. "He saw himself as my knight in shining armour. It was hard for him to deal with the truth."

And there was no doubt in my mind that my "uncle's" reckless mood that afternoon had played a pivotal role in how I ended up being a drug lord.

I still hadn't discovered the full story, but at least I was getting closer to it, now.

* * *

My father never came back to see my mother in hospital that afternoon. I didn't blame him. He'd been the keeper of so many of her secrets for too long, and my mother speaking in German had understandably been the last straw for him. My mother said she'd always wanted to apologize to him for everything that had happened between them, although now she realized it was too late.

She looked exhausted after telling me all this. Moments later, she began drifting in and out of consciousness just like she had on the first day I saw her. I did wonder for a few brief moments if everything she'd told me was just a series of death-bed hallucinations, fuelled by all her medication, but really it all made sense.

I sat by her bedside, gently clasping her hand for ages in complete silence. Then I felt her squeeze me back surprisingly tightly.

"He'll be back soon," she whispered, opening her eyes and looking at me a bit like a naughty child.

I tried to smile at her, although it wasn't easy after everything she'd just told me.

"He always comes back in the end," she said, as she tried to lift her shaking hand off the bed.

I didn't know what she was trying to do, so I picked up a plastic cup of water on the bedside table and passed it to her. Struggling for breath, she pushed it away and grabbed hold of the drip attached to her other arm and pulled it out, almost knocking over the stand next to her bed. After she'd done it, she smiled at me, once again like a naughty child.

I didn't call the nurse. I felt she had the right to make that decision all by herself. Instead, I held her hand tightly again and waited for her eyes to close. She'd soon be finally at peace with the world.

* * *

Outside the hospital, I was in a complete daze as I waited for a taxi. I'd just allowed my mother to end her own life, and in the cold light of day I was starting to regret having done so. Should I have stopped her? It wouldn't have been hard to do.

As I wrestled with all this, a silver BMW pulled up alongside me. I barely noticed it at first. Then the passenger side window rolled down and my old boss's widow smiled up at me. Next to her was the Cuban. I thought about telling them to fuck off, but I had nothing against them, really. I accepted their offer of a ride back to my mother's villa, where I was staying.

During the journey, the Cuban made it clear that he was worried my return to Ibiza meant I was planning to start operating there again. I laughed when he said that and assured him I had no such intention. Next to him in the front passenger seat, my old boss's widow nodded in agreement as the Cuban spoke. She was clearly no longer the little wife with no idea about her husband's life of crime.

Then she turned towards me and asked me if I remembered how obsessed her husband had been with what had been on my uncle's MTB boat all those years earlier. I nodded, surprised that she would even bring it up.

"Is that why you're back?" she asked.

I was about to ask her what she meant, but instead, I told her the exact same thing I'd always said to her husband: that my uncle never dealt in drugs, so why would he have been carrying any on his MTB?

"I didn't say they were drugs," she said, as we turned into the driveway to my mother's villa. Then the Cuban looked at her sternly and she stopped talking.

As they dropped me off, I thanked them politely for the ride and they made a point of saying they would "be in touch again soon".

It felt as if I'd just leapt from the frying pan into yet another fire. I'd managed to escape the heat in DRWA to end up walking straight into something even more troubling in Ibiza. And all I really wanted by this stage was a quiet life.

CHAPTER TWENTY-THREE
SERIOUS CONSEQUENCES

A few hours after my mother died, I phoned the two Chileans I worked with in the DRWA to find out if the cartel's final shipment had arrived safely. One of their satellite phones was picked up by the DRWA army major, whose men had been due to unload the 707 after it landed. He told me the plane had been strafed with machine gun fire by rebel fighters as it came into land.

The DRWA major said the plane had managed a crash landing and one of the Chilean pilots had survived as the aircraft had slid to a halt in a mud flat. The rebels arrived at the scene and hauled the surviving pilot out of the cockpit, attached him by rope to the back of a pick-up truck and then dragged him to a nearby town, which was one of their strong-holds. He died en route and his battered body was dumped on a main road as a warning to the cartel to leave the DRWA. The major also added, almost as an afterthought, that both the Chilean cartel members based in the capital had been kidnapped and killed by rebel forces.

After telling me all this in a detached manner, the major said that he and his men still expected to be paid their bribes, despite the cocaine and cannabis being blown out of the sky. I didn't bother asking him why he'd been speaking to me on one of the Chileans' satellite phones, but I assured him that he'd be paid. I knew I needed to play for time, and this felt like the best way.

Unsure what to do, I called my best friend in London for advice on how to deal with the DRWA situation. It was a risk because we hadn't spoken in ages, but I didn't know who else to turn to. He was understandably angry with me at first, presuming that my main priority was the drugs and cash I'd left behind in his home country. I assured him that all I cared about was making sure no one paid for my mistakes with their lives.

His voice softened and he warned me not to go back to the DRWA. He said my name was on a rebel hit list and I'd most likely be executed if I returned, if his father didn't have me killed first. He also told me it hadn't been the rebels who'd shot the cartel's 707 down but soldiers loyal to the president. He'd found out I'd left the country and decided to get rid of the cartel after the Chechen drug cartel connected to his new personal assistant had approached him with a much more lucrative deal to run the DRWA as a narco-state. So I guess I was screwed either way.

* * *

An hour later, the fax machine at my mother's villa fired up and six photographs appeared. They all showed the NGO woman and I out together holding hands on the streets of the DRWA just before she'd been killed. They'd been faxed from a phone number in Chile.

Minutes later, my satellite phone rang. It was La Princesa accusing me of colluding with the president to deliberately have her plane shot down and steal her shipment of cocaine and cannabis. She also asked why I had left the DRWA without her agreement.

Before I even had a chance to tell her about my mother, she claimed she'd found out from a corrupt DEA agent in Chile that the woman I'd been seeing had been working undercover for them. He'd identified her from photos La Princesa had taken. Her coldly pointed out she'd only had me followed in the first place to make sure I wasn't cheating on her.

So with nothing whatsoever to lose, I asked her if she'd had the NGO woman murdered. Her answer was to coldly point out that if she'd known earlier about the woman being a DEA agent, she would never have sent that final shipment over and that it was all on me. She wanted me to pay her $5 million, which was the full value of the cocaine lost when her plane was shot down, or, she said, there would be "serious consequences".

There was clearly nothing I could say which would convince her otherwise, so I changed the subject.

"How's your husband's cancer?"

"What?" she asked.

"I heard he was sick."

"That's none of your fucking business."

Then the phone line went dead.

Falling out with her should have been scary. But I was beyond fear by this stage. My life was so precariously balanced that my only priority was survival. I just had to hope I could avoid the landmines and make it to the other side.

CHAPTER TWENTY-FOUR
PICKING UP THE PIECES

My mother had expressly told me before she died that she didn't want a proper funeral service. Just her ashes scattered in the sea close to the rice fields near where she and my uncle had escaped from that prison camp, and close to where the MTB had gone down in that storm.

It was fortunate her demands were so modest because virtually all the most important characters in her life were already dead anyway. The New Zealander was the only survivor from the civil war. He'd kept a fatherly eye on me after my mother's death and made sure I wasn't too isolated by regularly popping round to see me with some food.

On the day we'd decided to sprinkle her ashes in the sea, I arranged to meet him at the secret beach. After we'd chatted for a while, I asked him why people like the Cuban and my old boss's widow were – after so many years – still obsessed with what my uncle's MTB had been carrying when it sank. He didn't look surprised by the question and suggested we walk up to the abandoned village behind the beach because he had something to show me before we went out to sea to scatter my mother's ashes.

As we climbed the rocks and the rundown village came into sight, the New Zealander explained the village's importance to my mother, my uncle and all the other International Brigades veterans.

"We all knew what happened there and we were determined to make sure no one ever forgot about it," he said.

"Your uncle was the one who convinced me to buy it in the first place. He even put some money towards it," said the New Zealander. "We were all a bit in awe of him back then."

I asked him if the abandoned village was connected to what my uncle had been doing in Ibiza when he turned up that afternoon on the MTB with Smelter and Shorty. The New Zealander sighed and said yes it was, but that it all went back to the civil war, like most things when it came to my family's past. He explained that when my uncle and mother had been imprisoned on that ship docked at Ibiza Old Town port, my uncle had noticed a Guardia Civil unit from Madrid – who'd travelled on the same vessel from the mainland – unloading wooden boxes, which dockers were expressly being forbidden from going anywhere near. Printed on the side of those boxes was the company name of "Braun" and "Munich". He recognized it as a Jewish gold dealer he himself had done business with in Germany in the mid-1930s.

But the day after the gold was unloaded in the port, the Guardia Civil unit handling it was wiped out when a boat they were travelling in back to the mainland was attacked by republican forces. They'd never even had a chance to tell Franco where they put his gold.

My uncle ended up spending the following 30 years on its trail, which explained why he kept visiting us in Ibiza during my childhood. He even established that Hitler had given the gold to his friend Franco as a thank you in advance for the Spanish staying neutral throughout the Second World War.

In early 1975 – with Franco on his deathbed – the old chief on Ibiza was ordered by his fascist superiors in Madrid to destroy all evidence of atrocities on the island during and after the civil war, in case a new democratically elected Spanish government prosecuted the nationalists as war criminals. The now elderly Guardia Civil chief knew that at least 50 republican prisoners, including members of the International Brigades, had been executed and then buried in a makeshift mass grave next to the bullring on the outskirts of Ibiza Old Town, so he ordered his men to dig up all the remains and incinerate them elsewhere. When they couldn't find them, the chief ordered that the entire stadium be torn down until the bodies were located. And while digging beneath the main auditorium, his men eventually stumbled on that gold bullion, still in the same boxes marked "Braun".

The chief immediately had it taken to a secure storage warehouse just off the main highway that ran across the island. He wanted the gold for himself but didn't know how to turn it into cash, so he sought out the advice of the British gangster (who later became my boss) who'd been bribing the old chief for years in order to smuggle cannabis onto the island. The gang boss said he knew a British expert called "Smelter" in London, who'd be the ideal man for the job.

Smelter also happened to be one of my uncle's best friends and he told my uncle all about the approach by the Brit. It was music to my uncle's ears after decades of trying to find the gold himself. Smelter and my uncle went into partnership with the Brit and they hatched a plan to steal the gold. That's why my uncle sailed over on his MTB with Smelter. They were due to meet the chief in Ibiza to inspect the gold before smelting it down in order to turn it into cash.

But the chief wasn't stupid. He was suspicious of Smelter right from the start, even though at that stage he had no idea about his connection to my uncle. It was only after much debate and a lot of cognacs that Smelter was finally blindfolded and taken by the chief to the warehouse to examine the gold. My uncle and his sidekick Shorty secretly shadowed them there.

During a meeting later that evening with the Brit, my uncle and Smelter fell out with him over how to divide the gold up once they'd stolen it. So my uncle and his two-man MTB crew moved fast and raided the warehouse in the middle of that same night and stole all the gold for themselves. They loaded it onto the MTB and sailed straight to the New Zealander's beach.

The New Zealander said he tried to convince my uncle to take the gold back to the warehouse because he thought it would cause them nothing but trouble once the chief found out what had happened. The New Zealander had spent years trying to placate the Guardia Civil, and particularly the old chief. But my uncle, Smelter and Shorty ignored the New Zealander's pleas and insisted on keeping the gold. They even cracked open some bottles of vintage cognac in the dusty bar of the abandoned village to celebrate.

The day after the robbery, my uncle turned up in his MTB at the beach with his two-man crew. When the chief saw Smelter with my uncle, he immediately suspected what had happened. So he went back down to his patrol boat on the jetty and radioed his officers in Ibiza Old Town to go to the warehouse to see if there had been a break-in. After he got confirmation of the robbery, he deliberately left the beach and sailed his Guardia Civil patrol boat out of the bay knowing the MTB would soon depart. He planned to shadow the vessel until it got into international waters. Then he'd raid it, kill my uncle and his two-man crew and recover the gold.

By this time, the New Zealander and I had reached the crumbling, overgrown square of the abandoned village, where I knew that communist fighters who had been held in the nearby prison camp had been tortured and executed. In the searing heat, with cicadas chirping around us, the New Zealander led me to the far corner of the square.

"But your uncle was a clever bastard," he said, as we walked. "He knew the chief would presume the gold was on the MTB when he turned up at the beach the following day saying he was off to Tangiers."

The New Zealander explained he'd been the only person apart from my uncle, Smelter and Shorty who knew where the gold was actually hidden. He'd even promised my mother he'd never touch it because she lived in hope that my uncle was still alive and that one day he'd come back for what he considered to be "his" gold.

We'd stopped walking just next to the crumbling wall outside the church, when the New Zealander began digging the toe of his flip-flops into the sand just like he used to do in his beach bar when I was a kid. But instead of peseta coins popping up, he kicked away enough sand and dirt to expose a small trap door in the ground. Looking down at it, he explained it was a solitary confinement cell for Republican prisoners. "We all spent time down there when we were in the camp, so we knew exactly where it was," he said.

Now my mother was no longer with us, the New Zealander wanted to get rid of the gold once and for all. And I knew he was right.

* * *

Later that day, we took a small boat from the jetty at the secret beach and headed out beyond the bay into the same stretch of the Mediterranean where so much of this story has unfolded. As the stinging heat of the sun gradually dispersed in a warm breeze, a narrow band of hazy mist hung just above the surface of the sea. I noticed some Medusa jellyfish drifting past the boat while we chugged gently out towards the open waters.

Five minutes later, the New Zealander turned off the engine and we bobbed around on the rippling water in almost complete silence, except for the sea gently lapping against the boat's wooden hull. I picked up an urn containing my mother's ashes from next to the helm and twisted the top off carefully. Then I tilted it out over the edge of the boat and let her ashes flutter over the surface of the sea in the breeze while the New Zealander looked on.

Once the urn was empty, he nodded at me and leaned down to open one of three identical wooden boxes with the name "Braun" and "Munich" stamped on them. Then we took it in turns to gently drop that tainted gold, one small brick at a time, into the water. We watched as each glistening ingot sank past the dancing jellyfish and into the deep, dark unknown.

After I'd dropped the last gold bar in the water, the New Zealander unscrewed the top of a jug of sangria and splashed some gin from a bottle into it. He gave it a quick stir with a spoon before pouring it into two stemmed glasses. We toasted my mother before throwing the same glasses into the sea along with the rest of the gin and sangria.

A few minutes later – as we chugged around the corner alongside the perimeter cliffs back into the bay in front of the secret beach – I noticed a big white powerboat tied up at the wooden jetty. As we got nearer, the Cuban and my old boss's widow emerged from the cabin. I looked at the New Zealander and he sighed. We both knew why they were there.

As we moved alongside their vessel at the dock, the Cuban stood on the ramshackle wooden jetty watching us. When I threw a rope, he grabbed it and tied it up expertly. I glanced across at the New Zealander again and then at the widow, who was now standing alongside the Cuban as we got off the boat.

"It's all gone now," I said, before either of them had a chance to say anything. "It'll never hurt anyone else again."

The widow looked at me suspiciously.

"How do I know you're not lying?" she finally said.

"Because you know that I'm not that sort of person," I answered.

She looked at the New Zealander and then back at me before grabbing hold of the Cuban's hand.

"If we find out you've still got it, we'll be back," she said, before turning to walk across the jetty towards the powerboat.

The New Zealander and I stood and watched as they boarded the vessel. The widow fired up the twin outboard engines while the Cuban untied the ropes at each end before throwing them onto the boat and jumping nimbly onto the deck.

Moments later, the widow reversed expertly out of the jetty area before turning and smiling at me as she pulled the throttle back gradually and the powerboat's long nose lifted out of the water as it surged towards the open seas.

I knew she'd worked out it was time to finally move on. And maybe I knew that too.

EPILOGUE
FULL CIRCLE

There was no chilling reprisal from La Princesa and her husband in the end. I never heard another word from either of them. The Cuban – whom I eventually became surprisingly friendly with despite our earlier differences – said he'd made sure that the Chilean cartel learned that I worked for the DEA, and La Princesa had presumably decided it wasn't worth the risk to send a hit team to Ibiza to deal with me. I thanked the Cuban for his overt disinformation, until he pointed out that he'd mainly said that so I could never work in the drugs trade again, as no one would ever deal with me if there was any suggestion that I had links to the DEA.

A few days later, I got a call from a woman with a South American Spanish accent. She sounded very nervous and claimed to be a friend of La Princesa. She said that she wanted me to know she deeply regretted telling her husband about us and that he'd turned out not to be the person she'd thought he was.

I never found out what the caller meant by that comment because the phone line cut off and no one ever rung back. Some months later, I read an article in a British newspaper that referred to a female Chilean drug cartel leader being murdered in a gang war between rival cartels. No name was given, so I don't know to this day if that was her.

* * *

Back in the DRWA, everything went up in flames, just as my old best friend had predicted. Eventually, he persuaded his father to abandon his homeland, along with the Chechen cocaine cartel who planned to set up an operation there.

My best friend once compared drug cartels to the blood-thirsty European colonials who'd ruined so many countries on the African continent through their greed, racism and brutality. He was right, of course, but I did feel like there was one difference: we'd been stopped in our tracks. These days, I fully accept a lot of the responsibility for what happened in the DRWA. The cartel effectively poisoned those corrupt politicians and public officials and conveniently side-stepped the plight of the people on the streets.

My best friend eventually announced plans to run for president himself after pledging that he was not in any way like his father and just wanted peace and prosperity for his homeland. Having departed the DRWA in a hurry, I'd left a fortune in cash hidden in that warehouse in the capital, which I told my best friend about. I wanted him to use it for his election campaign. It didn't make up for all the damage we'd caused the DRWA, but at least it might help a bit. We even joked that I would make an ideal personal assistant if he became president because of my previous knowledge of the DRWA. But he never took me up on my kind offer.

I heard the Americans believed my old friend would be more friendly towards them than the Marxist main opposition party, who wanted to take over from his father and forge closer links with the Chinese. The Americans asked my friend to assure them that if he did get elected then he would allow the DEA to set up a field office in the capital from where they could monitor all of the DRWA's problematic neighbours.

* * *

About a year after my mother died, the New Zealander – by this time in his late eighties – announced plans to return to his homeland, where his cousin had found him an old folks' home to reside at. He insisted on signing away the entire beach and abandoned village to me, on the condition that I never allowed the village to be demolished.

I'd already made sure all my connections to the drug game had been carefully erased by hiring a forensic accountant to help me clean the stash of cash I'd hidden behind my mother's villa and sell off what few properties I still owned in London. I used some of the remaining cash to purchase one of the last ever workable MTB boats from an old navy captain living in Shoreham-by-Sea, on the south coast of England. He kindly sailed it over to Ibiza and moored it at the end of the old wooden jetty in front of the secret beach, and I turned it into a restaurant. The walls are adorned with photos of International Brigades members, including my uncle, my mother, the New Zealander and all the rest. I called the restaurant "Smelter's".

I've continued to ensure the beach lives up to its "secret" reputation by refusing to tarmac the rocky old track to town, and the local fishermen are restricted to four return boat trips a day, so that limits the number of visitors.

About a year after I took it over, a global hotel chain tried to buy all the land to turn it into a five-star resort for the sort of tourists who've supposedly transformed Ibiza into the world's most popular party destination. The developers got quite heavy about it, and their lawyers even questioned the validity of the New Zealander's bequest to me, which had resulted in my inheriting the land. In the end, I obtained a court injunction against them on the basis that the abandoned village was a war monument, which could not be disturbed under any circumstances.

Luckily, the Guardia Civil these days are a much more peace-loving bunch than they used to be. They were keen to be seen to be backing me up on all fronts, especially when it came to rejecting the hotel plan. I'm still astonished the force wasn't completely disbanded after Franco died, but there are no further remnants from the civil war running things anymore, so it's fine. This new generation of friendly officers know they'll always be offered a cognac whenever they turn up at the secret beach on one of their brand-new, high-tech, cigar-shaped patrol powerboats.

Meanwhile, the Cuban didn't even get upset when I rejected his kind offer to pay me to use the secret beach as a place to drop off smuggled drugs. I didn't feel I was being disloyal to my old boss by continuing to be friendly with the Cuban, because that gold had proved to me that my boss had an ulterior motive in turning me into a drug gangster in the first place. I've never asked the Cuban if he played a direct role in killing the Brit, but I learned long ago that in this game it's better not to confront the past.

The son of my old boss eventually took over the island's main drug operation from the Cuban. That was probably the only moment when I felt a twinge of guilt. After all, I'd always admired the way my boss had gone out of his way not to tell his wife and children about his life of crime. But all that meant nothing now. Ibiza may well get dangerous again, which could mean trouble for my old boss's son.

A lot of mainly Irish and Eastern European gangsters are today moving into many of the main resort areas. Meanwhile, supposedly upmarket drug dealers from as far afield as London and Frankfurt fly in every summer to sell their narcotics during the busy tourist season to their regular customers. This new generation of drug dealers see Ibiza as nothing more than a territory they can take full advantage of. None of them understand or appreciate the history of the island and its connections to the past, including the civil war. They are the complete opposite of the old hippies like me who ruled the drugs underworld in our tie-dye shirts and flip-flops.

* * *

And me, I'm just so pleased to have stepped back from it all. One of the best things about ending my life of crime was that my father came to live with me back on Ibiza. He'd split with his German wife and – then in his late eighties – he announced that he wanted us to have some time together before it was too late.

A few days after he arrived on the island, I mentioned that I had a copy of the outline that the Hollywood director had written and presented to my mother on the beach all those years earlier. I thought he'd be upset by it, but he put on his old journalist's hat and announced that it was a barnstorming story and that we should try and turn it into a film script.

I'd never seen my father so happy. I think he found working on the script to be a cathartic experience, even though we bickered nonstop about the contents. My father wanted the story to cover all the way to that day when I dropped those gold bars into the sea with the New Zealander. I wasn't so sure. I felt my mother and uncle were the ones who'd made the sacrifices and that it should just be their story, which was hard for my father to accept, although he did in the end.

I eventually found a Hollywood agent to represent the script and it was sent out to several studios. Unfortunately, we never ended up getting a deal, and my father died soon after that. However, that story helped provide the unique backbone for this book.

* * *

These days I give guitar lessons for free in the favela just north of Ibiza Old Town. Tourists rarely venture there because it's not as picturesque as much of the rest of the island. Most of my pupils are local kids who can't afford to buy their own guitars, so I often give them one as long as they can prove to me they have a genuine interest in playing.

I'm trying to give something back to the island, although it sounds a bit pretentious to say it like that. I prefer to think I'm using all my experience, not just of guitar playing but of life itself, to help these kids work out a way to shape their future because I feel as if I owe this island something.

I still visit the old buildings and barren sites where others once stood and where some suffered appallingly during and after the civil war. They continue to represent the wildly contrasting sides of this magical place.

Franco's impending death in 1975 led to the demolition of the bullring and the Guardia Civil's 1930s-built police station. The prison camp had been destroyed in the 1950s. All this had been supposed to help hide the fascists' many war crimes.

And every time there's a storm, I think back to what happened to my uncle and how it influenced my entire life. There is no getting away from the fact that if I'd never got on that MTB boat before it sailed off into those huge waves then I'd probably have ended up selling a bit of pot here and there and spending much of my life as my mother's carer. I wouldn't have seen the world and I'd most probably have taken far too many drugs to try and kill the boredom of my life. So in a way, I'm glad.

AFTERTHOUGHTS

The life and habits of the fragile yet dangerous Medusa jellyfish who've gracefully floated through so many significant moments of my story epitomize the journey I've taken throughout my life. Like them, I've drifted in and out of trouble, rarely fully connecting with stuff but managing to work my way around most obstacles without inflicting too much harm.

Jellyfish always give the appearance they don't give a shit, when the opposite is actually true. They're constantly having to navigate dangerous territorial waters to survive. There have been many times when I haven't taken responsibility for my actions and swerved around a problem because I didn't like people trying to second-guess me. It's led to countless close shaves, high risks and tainted relationships, but somehow I've survived it all, just like the jellyfish who drift past most things instead of confronting them. It usually helps them avoid any permanent damage and, beyond some mental scars, I've mostly managed to do the same.

The notion of all things in life being connected was definitely relevant to my survival and what ultimately saved me from prison or death or both. These connections began with my parents and ended with the New Zealander, I suppose. But all those people in the middle whom you've just read about played their own unique roles in this story. This all helped me develop the mental toughness that enabled me to survive.

I thought I was a good person until after my "uncle's" MTB sank on that fateful afternoon and I discovered there's no such thing as good or bad people. We all have another side to our character, even if only a few of us ever have an opportunity to recognize it. The trouble is that once you open up that bad side, it becomes a never-ending battle to ensure the good side stays one step ahead of it. These days, I reckon it's fine to let the bad side win now and again but just not too often.

I often laugh out loud at the irony that the gold I knew nothing about for more than three decades trapped me in a criminal life. But it's not so unusual. When you talk to most real-life criminals, they usually struggle to come up with a genuine reason for having become gangsters in the first place. Many fell into the underworld by accident and then found themselves with no easy route out of it.

The one thing I cannot put behind me are the constant nightmares. I've learned to turn their darkness into something positive because they sometimes feature the main characters from my real-life story, who're no longer with us. I actually enjoy "meeting" those people and I always wake up before anything really bad happens to them.

I'm proud about never getting directly involved in any violence throughout my career in crime, though. I have no doubt that the bad karma caused by hurting others would have caught up with me in the end and I wouldn't be here talking to you now.

I hope that, having read my story, you'll appreciate why I still don't – to this day – consider myself a natural criminal. After all, I could easily have taken all that gold when it finally came into my hands. Instead, I recognized the death and destruction it had caused and knew that it had to be destroyed forever before it took down any more innocent victims. I'd also given my word to the New Zealander, and he'd given me his empire as part of that deal.

I've always believed that you have to take every opportunity that comes your way or else you will be destined to a life of regret. That doesn't mean there should be no regrets along the way, though. My biggest one is without doubt the death of my Chilean girlfriend. The fact she ended up working for a cocaine cartel doesn't negate the tragedy of her life. She had little choice in what she could do in order to feed and clothe her poverty-stricken family back in her war-torn homeland. I'd believed from the very first moment we'd met that we'd end up together for the rest of our lives, and her cold-blooded murder sent my own life spiralling even more out of control than it already was.

I'm also still filled with remorse about the murder of that NGO woman in the DRWA. She wasn't DEA, as La Princesa had claimed. I'm haunted by the realization that she died because of me.

On the other hand, my romance with La Princesa bewilders and appals me to this day. It seems to have been built around mutual loneliness and a need to escape – albeit temporarily – from the criminal world we both inhabited. But that is no excuse for allowing myself to be pulled into a toxic, twisted supposed love affair punctuated by death, deceit and destruction. All the so-called rules about relationships went out the window with La Princesa.

She had the blood of at least three participants in this story on her hands – her own father, my boss and the old chief. And she so nearly also cost me my life.

DEDICATION

My mother and her International Brigades friends were like heroes to me when I was a child. I grew up with a somewhat romantic vision of the civil war and all the horrors that revolved around it, even though I knew so little about what actually happened to her. Even when I finally learned that my mother made that huge and life damaging sacrifice to ensure my uncle and her weren't executed, it took nothing away from my feelings of awe and admiration when it came to her extraordinary life.

She taught me to be courageous and never to judge someone by their outward appearance. Also, I learned from her to dig deep to discover the inner soul of a person.

Today I often wander through the olive groves near my mother's beloved villa on my own trying to get to grips with everything that happened to her and how it led me to this place. I've concluded that her death effectively helped free me from the underworld completely. And that gold could only be finally liberated after she died because the New Zealander had promised not to touch it before she went.

Her uncompromising attitude helped give me the freedom to survive outside the normal world. She often encouraged me to see myself as an idealistic hippy, who could somehow live off the land without the usual financial obsessions.

So whatever way I look at it, most roads seem to lead back to my mother.

I dedicate this book to her. May she rest in peace.

We're all golden sunflowers inside.
Allen Ginsberg